Reviving Your Romance

40 Days to a Better Marriage

Devotional Study Guide
with audio listening CDs

by Terry & Barbi Franklin

TYLIS
PUBLISHING
Nashville, Tennessee

REVIVING YOUR ROMANCE
Published by Tylis Publishing, Inc.

© 2005 by Terry & Barbi Franklin
Cover design by Jennifer Allison of www.agpdesign.com

Printed in the United States of America

For information:
TYLIS PUBLISHING
P.O. Box 17247
Nashville, TN 37217-0247
USA
615-773-8480

Library of Congress Cataloging-in-Publication Data

Franklin, Terry and Barbi
Reviving Your Romance (40 Days To A Better Marriage) / Terry and Barbi Franklin
p. cm.
ISBN # 0-9778908-0-5
1.   Marriage – Prayer-books and devotions – English. I. Franklin, Robert T. 1957- II. Franklin, Barbara J. 1959- Reviving Your Romance.
TX 6-324-354 2006
Second Printing

This book is dedicated to:

Dr. James & Donna Murk

for the impact they have made
on our marriage, as well as countless other families in
over 50 years of marriage and ministry worldwide.

You're the best parents and parents-in-law
a couple could ever have!

❧ Thank You's ❧

We want to take a moment to thank the friends, family,
and prayer warriors who helped make this book possible!

Mom, Sandy Greenway, you were faithful to be an encouragement
throughout the entire process of writing and editing this devotional. Thank
you for taking so much of your time to bless us in this way!

Friends and family members as well as our prayer team members that
continue to pray for us and are an encouragement to us and this ministry:

Ed & Heidi Lamberg
Graziella Giannetta
Don & Gypsie Arnold
Don & Patti McCain
Jerry & Pat Mercer
Colin & Lori Ireton
Steve & Annie Chapman
Our two precious sons, Tyler and Travis Franklin
Bob & Sue Franklin for your encouragement
Brienne Murk, for your great ideas, and
all our faithful, praying family members, especially
Beverly Murk, and good friends: Trish, and Becki, as well as
all our other prayer team members around the country.

Thanks to Jennifer Allison of agpdesign.com for the great cover design, and
Keith Sealy, for engineering and mixing, and
Tim Parton, for bringing the audio CDs to life with your keyboard.

Also, thanks to North Park Church. Your commitment to do this
devotional study with all your couples in advance of publication was the
encouragement and catalyst to complete this book in a timely manner.

We pray that all of you who go through this book will gain wisdom,
understanding, and knowledge that will benefit your marriage for a lifetime!

May God richly bless you, your marriage, and your family!

Introduction

$\mathcal{T}$he marriage covenant is not only the most important earthly relationship God created, but it's also the most complicated. Unlike casual friendships, marriage is a powder-keg of vulnerability, eliciting emotions of love one moment... and contrasting explosive ones the next. Careful study of what makes a good marriage is essential, for when our marriages are healthy and strong there is a far greater chance that our families will be strong. If multiplied many times, the same could be said for our churches, cities and nation.

Most would agree that prayer is vital to a godly marriage. But how many couples really pray together? In these next 40 days you will build a habit that will be a blessing to you now and for years to come. While there are no quick fixes to marriage problems, this devotional study guide will make a positive difference in your relationship as you and your mate seek the Lord together. The topics covered include common areas of conflict that many couples face.

Don't be surprised if this book occasionally agitates your emotions! If continual hurt has been buried within you for some time, it may trigger feelings that cause you desire to lash out at your spouse. We encourage you not to do that. Determine now that you are *for* each other; not *against* each other! As you pray together and work through this book, you'll begin to see positive changes. Humility and a teachable spirit will be your greatest assets and will lead you forward toward growth and maturity.

This devotional study guide is filled with basic practical living principles you can further develop and apply to your life and marriage. Once you've completed the 40 days, you may want to go back through the book as a refresher, or wait 6 months and do the study again after you've had time to assimilate things you have learned. You may also want to use the key verses as memory verses to learn together, even at a later time. One verse per week will have you well on your way to memorizing a year of powerful verses that will change your marriage.

Throughout this study, most of the scripture verses are in the New International Version (NIV). If the verse is marked with another translation: eg. (NAS) or (NKJ), it means we used a translation other than the NIV for various reasons; often to reflect what we perceive to be a more accurate understanding of the original Greek or Hebrew language. We encourage you to read all the additional scriptures listed. They will strengthen your understanding of the principles being emphasized and enrich your spiritual growth. While it is sometimes hard to grasp the entire meaning of a verse (most of us can't read it in the original languages), God will help *you* apply His Word, if you ask Him to.

Every couple has a different schedule and routine. The effort you make in carving out time in your schedule will determine the success of this study. You could make plans to meet in the morning, or during dinner preparations, or even before bedtime. If one of you has to travel, use the audio CD and then "meet" by phone. Make plans to stay connected even if it's only 10 minutes a day. Don't panic if you miss a day. Just pick up where you left off. God's desire is that you experience all He created marriage to be: a satisfying relationship like no other. He wants to bless you so that you, in turn, can be a blessing to the world.

Before you launch into the Study, we want to establish some suggested ground rules for your discussions:

Ground rule #1: While we are dealing with areas of common conflict in marriages on some of these pages, every effort should be made to *keep the atmosphere POSITIVE.*

Ground rule #2: *Invite God to be a part of your conversations.* He wants to empower you to live in unity and cause you and your mate to not only be lovers, but best friends. Yes, it can happen – don't give up!

Ground rule #3: If the conversation begins to heat up, *take a break for a while until emotions settle* and the subject can be discussed without unkind words. (This indicates an area of need that God wants to heal.)

Ground rule #4: As we said before, *determine that you are FOR each other, not AGAINST each other.*

When you see this *explosive* sign: 💣 it indicates a potentially volatile question – great care should be given in your response. ALL marriages have areas of disagreement. Years of marriage can sometimes cause these areas to grow quite large. The explosive icon is apropos, because bombs can blow up. Be humble and open without accusing your spouse or becoming defensive regarding their perspective. You may retreat to simply *"agree to disagree,"* but you should still listen to each other's perspectives. There is usually a valid reason your spouse feels the way they do. Stay open, and be willing to apologize. None of us are perfect...

We believe that after you and your mate finish this study, you'll be able to bring another couple, or even several couples, through this study and spread the blessing around. Many married couples are looking for some encouragement in their marriage, and you could be the very people God uses to help them. May God richly bless you and your marriage as you begin this devotional study! Now let's start our journey...

– Terry & Barbi Franklin

Important Note: If either you or your spouse struggle with substance abuse of any type, we recommend your getting immediate help to overcome your addiction. Rehabilitation and counseling for addictions is necessary before confronting marital conflicts, as substance abuse alters the mind and emotions of the abuser. Most marriage counselors recognize that therapy is not effective in resolving marital issues until addictions are overcome. But we still hope you will read this devotional and all scriptures listed, as the truth of God's Word and its principles will help to bring freedom and deliverance.

"By wisdom a house is built, by understanding it is established, by knowledge its rooms are filled with rare and beautiful treasures."
Proverbs 24:3-4

Did you know that there is a treasure chest right inside the front door of your house? You can be dirt-poor and yet incredibly wealthy as a couple, because, often the riches that God gives are priceless; the kind that money can't buy. God wants you to have a GREAT marriage. And He knows how to get you there. But sometimes we don't trust that the Inventor of this institution knows what He's doing.

One night when our boys were restless little toddlers, one of them began complaining about being hungry only five minutes before dinner time. Even though he'd been told that dinner was almost ready, he continued to whine. Finally, when he didn't see food magically appear immediately after his inquiry, he ran into the living room screaming, *"Mommy doesn't love me any more... supper is never going to be ready... wahhhhh!"*

We were surprised at the thought that our son would ever question our desire to give him everything we could, especially dinner! But isn't that like many of us, even as adults. Somehow, we don't understand how very deeply our Father in Heaven loves us and longs to not only meet our basic needs, but bless us as well.

As the Creator of the universe, it was God who invented romance. But heaven's Sovereign also has another unique quality: He knows how to get romance back. A careful reading of the "Song of Solomon" in the Bible bears this out. Although it has been perverted by the world, we should never forget that even the sexual intimacy between a husband and wife was His idea.

As we grow together and allow God to teach us, we can build a home and marriage that is a Fort Knox of security, resistant to outer pressures, but having the *gold* of a priceless relationship within. In Genesis 18:18-19, God called Abraham and his family to preserve and guard His ways by teaching and following them. God made a covenant with Abraham and told him that He not only wanted to bless him, but also use him and his family to bless the nations of the world. But that blessing didn't stop with him!

You are called by God, too. If you are a Christian, those blessings are available for YOU, too! In fact, the scriptures show that Calvary's Cross ushered in a new covenant that is even better than the one he made with Abraham (Hebrews 7:22). YOUR marriage and family has the potential of becoming a blessing to the world! While it's true that politicians may not always tell the truth, you can trust that every promise in the Bible is for you. And God is always faithful to keep His Word.

In Hebrews 6:17, the original Greek language expresses God's *"exceeding, abundant"* and *"affectionate desire"* to *"prove"* to us the *"unchangeable"* nature of the promises He has given to us. His will, purpose, and destiny for our marriages and families is far greater than we could ever comprehend.

As you pursue Him together through this devotional, our prayer is that God will bring healing to the broken places in your marriage. As you passionately seek Him as husband and wife, He will reveal truths that will increase your romantic love, unity and all the rare and priceless treasures that will bless you as a couple. These blessings can then flow through you to touch the world.

Look-up Scriptures:
Genesis 18:18-19   Isaiah 30:18   Galatians 3:6-9
Prov. 2:1-6; 8:17-21   Jeremiah 29:11-13   Hebrews 6:17-18

Questions to Ask Myself:
Am I putting as much effort into mining the "treasure" from my marriage as I am the other lesser "riches" in my life?

Questions to Ask Each Other:
Do you feel like our "romance" could be better than it is? Are you willing to pray together these next 40 days for those "rare and beautiful treasures" God gives those who seek Him?

Prayer: Lord, fill us with a new and fresh desire to seek you and your Word. We want to find the riches and abundance in our marriage that you intend for us to have. Teach us how to mine valuable treasure through this devotional study guide. Revive and increase our romance so we can have the best marriage possible.

"Do not let any unwholesome talk come out of your mouths, but only what is helpful for building others up according to their needs, that it may benefit those who listen." Ephesians 4:29

When our kids were very young they would occasionally argue with each other, as siblings sometimes do. One of them would want a toy the other had, and would simply grab it out of the other's hand. Weeping, wailing, and gnashing of teeth would result. Then nasty words would follow. Then name calling and all the other typical things children do when they are fighting. Instead of merely stopping them, we added a positive action. We would have them speak blessings to each other. This doesn't come naturally to kids; neither is it an effortless exercise for husbands and wives.

As we attempted to teach our boys to get along and replace hurtful words with kind ones, we had them memorize Bible verses to help them see the importance of blessing each other. One useful scripture was Proverbs 12:18, *"Reckless words pierce like a sword, but the tongue of the wise brings healing."* Sometimes it didn't seem that they were connecting with the application of this verse. Even when asked to quote it in the middle of an argument, they would say the verse and then pick right up where their fight left off, saying more bad things to each other.

One day, in the middle of their fight, we made them hold their tongues – literally! Between their index finger and thumb, they held their tongues and quoted the verse, muffling the words incoherently. As funny as this episode sounds, it began to work! Eventually, when they started to speak unkindly to each other, even for a minute, all we'd have to do is peek in the door; they'd grab their tongues, muffle their verse and stop fighting.

It's sad that some of us never learned this lesson in our childhood, and many couples are still saying bad things to each other, creating wounds in each other's hearts that are hard to heal. Though we aren't children, we, as adults, can still act like them.

As husbands and wives, our words can either be as life-giving as water, or as lethal as a dagger. Ephesians 4:29 is critical for us to put into practice, particularly with our spouse. The original Greek describes the words *"unwholesome talk"* as *"rotten words"*. When something is rotten, it's worthless...and it stinks. It can even spread its decaying characteristics to anything it touches. When we speak worthless, wounding words to our spouse, infection can set in, creating an unhealthy atmosphere in our homes.

Notice the next exhortation in this verse.... to build others up "ACCORDING TO THEIR NEEDS!" Many couples would find a marked change in the climate of their homes if they would simply replace uncaring "bad" words with these "good" words of blessing that their spouse really needs to hear.

Thayer's translates these words of blessing as words that are *"good and honorable,"* that *"promote another's growth"* in a way that appropriately fits their *"needs," "ministering good-will, joy, and loving-kindness."* More than likely, no one knows your spouse better than you. You are in the best position to fulfill this critical need we all have to be blessed!

Look-up Scriptures:

Proverbs 10:19-21	Matthew 15:11-12	Philippians 2:4
Proverbs 14:1; 15:4	Luke 6:43-47	James 1:26; 3:5-11

Questions to Ask Myself:
Do I say words to my spouse that I myself would want to hear? Are my words creating a healthy atmosphere in our home? Have I developed any bad habits, even from my childhood, that are verbally destructive?

Questions to Ask Each Other:
What words of blessing would you like to hear me say? Are there words you would prefer not to hear? Describe what I can say to you that will build you up in a way that meets your needs.

Prayer: Lord, help us to be more aware of what we say to each other and how it affects the other. Give us wisdom and restraint to control the words we say so we don't tear each other down. Teach us by your Holy Spirit how to communicate in a way that ministers good-will, joy, and loving-kindness to one another.

"The thief comes only to steal and kill and destroy; I have come that they may have life, and have it to the full." John 10:10

Walk through any park in a major city and you'll catch the sight of human "love birds." Walking hand in hand, sitting by a fountain wrapped in an embrace, these couples want to spend all their time together. And if their love is true, they only want the very best for each other. This desire, to want what is best for the other person, attracts them to each other like a magnet.

Because of His great love, God wants the very best for each of us! He told us so, but He went so much further; by sending His only Son, who gave His life in our place so that we can have life... everlasting life... the *"absolute fullness of life,"* the life that He originally created us to have. In John 10:10, having life to the "full" means a life that's *"superabundant, extraordinary, and more remarkable"* than we could ever imagine. And it's not just meant for our future in heaven some day, but even now, while living for God here on earth. And that includes your marriage, too!

When you met your spouse, God saw that it was good. He even ordained it. But, you might say, *"That's impossible – we met at a bar when we were young, and we weren't even saved!"* Well, in a way we don't fully understand, God, in His sovereignty, knew all of that ahead of time. He is without equal in taking the broken pieces of our lives and shaping them into beautiful works of art. He not only wants your marriage to succeed, but He wants your relationship and romance to be extraordinary! He is completely <u>for</u> you and will provide everything you need for success; and that includes your most important relationship, your marriage.

The problem is that every marriage has an enemy, a demonic foe that doesn't want your love to grow or your marriage to work. The old saying, *"Ignorance is bliss,"* doesn't apply here. Not understanding that there is an enemy pursuing our destruction would be like going into battle without knowing anything about our adversary. The more we learn of our enemy's strategies, the better we are at winning.

In Ephesians 6:12, it says, *"For our struggle is not against flesh and blood, but against the rulers, against the authorities, against the powers of this dark world and against the spiritual forces of evil in the heavenly realms."* Usually when we have a conflict, we imagine we are fighting with our spouse. However, while not diminishing the part our flesh takes in our disputes, we need to beware of the powerful battle raging in the spirit realm to divide us. In fact, one of the meanings of the name devil is *"to divide without cause."* In the Greek, this struggle is likened to a *"hand-to-hand wrestling match,"* where the victor is decided *"by pinning his opponent by the neck with his own bare hands."* The devil is just sly enough to make us believe that our spouse is the enemy, so that he can *"steal"* our married bliss, *"kill"* our love, and *"destroy"* our unity (John 10:10).

Though the devil can be behind our conflicts, it is still our responsibility to control ourselves and respond to conflict in a godly way. The best way to win the fight with our enemy is to become not only knowledgeable about <u>his</u> strategies, but more importantly, about <u>God's</u> plan and will, which are all found in His Word. Even Jesus Himself said that the truth sets us free (John 8:32)... free from sin's darkness and the lies the enemy tries to impose on us. The truth of the Word of God brings freedom from bondage and gives life and hope.

Look-up Scriptures:
John 8:31-32   Galatians 5:1   James 4:7
II Corinthians 10:3-7   Hebrews 4:12   I Peter 5:7-10

Questions to Ask Myself:
When I'm in a conflict with my spouse, do I take responsibility to react in a godly way? Do I realize that the cause of the conflict may be our common enemy? Am I taking every thought captive to Christ and the truths of His Word?

Questions to Ask Each Other:
Will you pause to pray with me when we're in a conflict? At these times, will you remind me that we're on the same team?

Prayer: Lord, open our eyes to see clearly when the enemy is lying to us or creating division between us. Give us the strength to stand against him together and recognize his tactics.

"Pride goes before destruction, a haughty spirit before a fall." Proverbs 16:18

One of the hardest things in the world to do is to admit that we're wrong. Why? ...because it hurts our pride. Somehow, we want to believe that we are capable, even without God. We go to great lengths to stand up for ourselves and defend our greatness when, all along, we all know we're flawed human beings. One of the best gifts we can give our spouse is to have an attitude of humility!

Years ago, a very large church invited us to fly to their city and give a concert that they hoped would be an outreach to marriages and families. They put a lot of effort into promoting the event with radio and television advertisements, and major mail-outs to their community. They had sold tickets in advance and had even placed our names on a big marquee outside of the church. The crowd filled the seats, the lights were dimmed, and then the Master of Ceremonies gave a glowing introduction, informing the crowd of how great we were. (You feel like something is about to happen, don't you??)

There was only one problem: Terry was coming down with laryngitis. We didn't even know how bad it was until we got up on the stage and really began singing our songs. As the first song progressed, Terry sounded like he was going through puberty again! We stumbled through another song, but by the third song, even the crowd was snickering at us. It was humiliating.

Struggling through the night, unprepared for this, we told a few stories of God's provision and answers to prayer in our marriage and family, and finished with a closing prayer after only 45 minutes, asking people to commit their families to God and come forward to pray. As we walked off stage, we immediately met the sponsor who was walking toward us. Terry, figuring that he was upset, immediately said, *"We're so sorry. We'll give you your money back. I didn't realize I was so sick."* But as we looked at him, tears were running down his cheeks. *"Look!"* he said. As we turned around, we saw the front of the auditorium jammed with people weeping before God. Marriages were healed and families rededicated themselves to the Lord. Later, the sponsor told us that they had never had God move in their church like that before.

We should have been ecstatic at what God did, but our pride was wounded. We realized that night that God really didn't need our talent. He was able to pull it all off, even when we were at our worst. So, it really IS all about Him!

Unfortunately, God had to humble us through that difficult experience. I'm sure we needed it. But what God really wants is for us to humble ourselves, before we take a spill… before the dishonor or destruction comes. When we humble ourselves to God and to each other, He can mold us into all the things He wants us to be. If we defend ourselves in pride, God will often, lovingly, allow us to fall flat on our faces through the challenges of every day life!

Choose today to walk in a spirit of humility, open to God's Holy Spirit to teach you new things that will change your life and marriage forever. Ask the Lord today to give you, as a couple, humble attitudes and teachable hearts, and see what He will do!

Look-up Scriptures:
Proverbs 11:2   Isaiah 45:9-12   Matthew 20:25-28
Proverbs 13:10   Jeremiah 18:4-6   James 4:6

Questions to Ask Myself:
Do I let my pride get in the way of being a better husband/wife? Is my first reaction to humble myself when my spouse tries to share his/her concerns with me? Can I easily humble myself to put my spouse's needs first, or does selfish pride rise up to stop me?

Questions to Ask Each Other:
How should I best approach you when I'm bothered by your actions? Is there a best time/place for this? If you were in my shoes, describe what this approach would look like?

Prayer: Lord, give us the grace to humble ourselves so we can learn all that you desire to teach us. Strengthen us by your Spirit and your Word to be mature enough to admit when we're wrong and plant in us a desire to change. Give each of us a compassionate heart so that our apologies will come easier. Help us focus on You and Your perfection, not ours.

"...being strengthened with all power according to his glorious might so that you may have great endurance and patience..." Colossians 1:11

Kate and Phil had dated for several years before marriage, so they knew each other quite well. After their wedding, Kate had expected married life to be like a constant "slumber party" with her best friend. It didn't take long for her expectations to be frustrated.

Shortly after their honeymoon, Kate came home from a depressing day at work. A co-worker was jealous of her and was spreading malicious rumors behind her back. She was devastated and longed to tell Phil. He was always so good at listening and understanding her. But that evening he had to work late to make up for time he had missed during their honeymoon. When he finally arrived home, he had a quick supper and they both prepared to turn in for the night. When Phil came to bed, Kate had propped herself up with her pillow... legs crossed... ready to talk.

As she began to pour out her heart, Phil plopped down, secretly annoyed and exhausted, with his head on his pillow. After only 5 minutes of giving a tear-filled, blow-by-blow account of her traumatic day, Kate heard a terrible noise... Phil had fallen asleep and was snoring! She was terribly hurt by his insensitivity. But this was only the beginning of their disappointments over the conflicting expectations they had for their marriage relationship.

Phil had expectations, too. He felt that his desire for love-making had been overlooked that night. Kate had been on his mind all day as he remembered those wonderful nights on their honeymoon. Driving home from work, he was playing drums on the steering wheel of his truck, singing, "Tonight's The Night," at the top of his lungs, like a redneck Rod Stewart. He was thinking, "I'm goin' home to my sweetie for some lovin'!" Neither received what they were hoping for. Two very different people – with two very different visions of married life – were now living under one roof. Their expectations would require something beyond themselves, because neither of them felt equipped to fulfill the other's desires. Their high expectations were driving them down a very rocky road.

Moses was a person with high expectations, too. When God called him to go lead His people out of the bondage of slavery in Egypt, *"Moses said to the Lord, 'O Lord, I have never been eloquent, neither in the past nor since you have spoken to your servant. I am slow of speech and tongue.' The LORD said to him, 'Who gave man his mouth? Who makes him deaf or mute? Who gives him sight or makes him blind? Is it not I, the LORD? Now go; I will help you speak and will teach you what to say'."* (Exodus 4:10-12) Moses thought it was all about his own ability; he expected too much of himself! By focusing on <u>himself</u>, he forgot that the Almighty always supplies the power to do what He requires. And that same power is available for our marriages.

Is your spouse not meeting some of your expectations? You might be tempted to give up in despair and stay perpetually frustrated. Often, when we blame our mate for not fulfilling our dreams, we forget that we have God's strength to draw from. <u>He will help us communicate our desires and empower us to fulfill each other's expectations</u>. This doesn't happen in a day. It takes time to grow in our understanding of our mate's desires. But with God's help we will learn to understand and meet our spouse's expectations and grow in an even stronger, more passionate love.

Look-up Scriptures:

Proverbs 19:11	I Corinthians 3:7	Colossians 1:9-12
Isaiah 40:28-31	Ephesians 4:15-16	James 1:2-8; 5:10-11

Questions to Ask Myself:
Am I willing to listen to my spouse explain his/her desires and expectations? Am I asking the Lord for the strength to be what my spouse needs? Am I patient enough to let my spouse grow?

Questions to Ask Each Other:
💣 If there are unmet expectations you would like to see fulfilled in our marriage, what would they be? How can I best meet those expectations? 💣 Do you need more "listening" time from me?

Prayer: Lord, strengthen us to fulfill each others expectations. Help us do things out of unselfish love. Fill us with your Spirit so we can be patient with each other as we learn the other's desires.

"So they are no longer two, but one. Therefore what God has joined together, let man not separate." Matthew 19:6

"Yes, but I was the one that made the decision to marry her. I didn't ask for God's permission! Don't bring Him into it. Listen, she's never going to change. I want a divorce!" said Roy. He was adamant that his 8-month marriage to Annie was not going to work and was firmly convinced that he had made a big mistake. Using a common excuse for divorce: that he was "backslidden" at the time of the wedding; Roy, like a man with his fingers crossed behind his back, felt like his marriage was never legitimate; never God's will. Unfortunately, you can't force someone to do what they don't want to do, and, sadly, Roy did divorce Annie.

But every couple is brought together by some "spark." That spark can be a variety of things. And sometimes a spark, in another area of the marriage, can cause a disaster... igniting flammable issues that can burn a relationship to the ground. Like Roy and Annie, these things can happen early in a marriage; but, like a spark lighting the end of a long fuse, they can happen many years later. Sometimes, even when a couple is many years into their marriage, something will trigger what ends in a final collapse of their relationship. One spouse will meet someone who they're convinced will better satisfy their needs, or when kids leave home and leave a void... there are multiple ways the enemy of our soul attempts to destroy God-ordained marriage.

We have to learn to get past our feelings. Most couples, at one time or another, feel that they have irreconcilable differences. Some even believe, like the example above, that God was never in agreement with their marriage, or that He can't help them fix their problems. But marriage was God's idea; He means for it to be a covenant commitment until we die. So, the crying actress telling of her recent divorce on the T.V. talk-show that says, *"I just knew it was time to look out for what was best for me..."* is <u>wrong</u>... regardless of the audience's approving by their spirited applause. The marriage covenant is not based on human philosophies or what is thought to be culturally or politically correct. We must go to God's Word to understand what God thinks of this commitment.

Malachi 2:16 declares that God hates divorce. Most people would agree. Everyone hates divorce! Ask innocent children caught in a tug of war between mommy and daddy. They hate divorce, too. A recent Barna poll showed that of the 35% of born-again Americans divorcing today, 23% have divorced twice!

What was the biggest problem Roy and Annie were facing? Feelings! Guess what, that dream you occasionally have about marrying someone else and things turning out different – every married person has the same dream at some time! They are just fickle feelings. God placed you with your mate to make you a better person. Proverbs 27:17 says, *"As iron sharpens iron, so one man sharpens another."* Two people become better for uniting their lives together. God uses this union to balance out our flaws and bring us to maturity in deeper love and wisdom. It's God's will for you to work out your problems and stay married.

Choose today to stand on God's truth, not feelings. Will you obey God and His Word and keep the everlasting covenant commitment to your wife/husband? He will give you the strength to fulfill the marriage vows you spoke and He ordained, and in the process, you will become a better person for it!

Look-up Scriptures:

Joshua 24:15	Proverbs 21:30	Matthew 19:3-6
Psalm 139:16	Malachi 2:16	Ephesians 1:11

Questions to Ask Myself:
Am I falling for the lie that says that my marriage wasn't really ordained by God? Am I willing to stand on the truth of God's Word no matter what my feelings tell me?

Questions to Ask Each Other:
How can we increase our understanding of what God's intentions for our marriage are? Are we willing to stand on God's truth and learn more about how to revive our love so we don't make foolish mistakes?

Prayer: Lord, we know you ordained our marriage. We want to learn how to make this marriage better so we aren't tempted to give up. Teach us how to fortify our commitment and romance.

7 ❧ Blessings of Bonding ᕗ 7

"If two lie down together, they will keep warm. But how can one keep warm alone?" Ecclesiastes 4:11

There are many practical reasons why God created the institution of marriage. But most importantly, He knew we need companionship – someone to do things together with, to love and live with. Imagine the joy that the Godhead felt during Creation; each member was involved working in union with the other. And it was this God who said it wasn't good for man to be alone. And most of us would agree.

Sometimes we get discouraged because our spouse doesn't share our same interests. In fact, there are some things that we enjoy that our spouse can hardly stand. We knew a happily married couple that began to lose interest in each other through the years because the wife always wanted to go shopping at the mall. When they were dating, and then when they married, he would traipse around behind her and act interested, but that soon ended. And now the thought of his having to walk in to a fabric shop would make him break out into a cold sweat.

The husband only wanted to sit on the couch and watch ESPN on television, something his wife greatly disliked. Instead of bonding, which happens naturally around common interests, they were drifting apart like two sailboats wandering away from their safe harbor. But they learned a valuable lesson in an odd place: on their family vacation.

The husband had another love: go-cart racing. When they got to their vacation spot, he took the family to every go-cart track he could find. But his son was the only one that shared this interest. His daughters were very upset, and put up with it for the first day, until he wanted to go back the next day, and the next. Mom and all the girls threatened to never go on a vacation with him again! They wanted to do something that they liked to do. Finally, they all sat down and talked about what each person wanted to do on their vacation, and they planned it so that each family member would get to do something that was fun for them.

Perhaps not every family would be able to come together quite like this, but certainly two people can manage to find

19

activities that are pleasing for both of them. Since our marriage is so important, experiencing rewarding and enjoyable times together is critical. Marriage therapists and counselors advise spending time every week doing mutually gratifying activities together. This encourages the bond we have with our spouse to continue to grow. This is not only good for our well-being in general, but it is especially critical if the couple is working to restore their marriage.

In the back of this devotional is a fun survey that you and your spouse can complete. It asks each of you to rate each of the recreational activities listed on a scale of 1 to 10 (1 meaning: greatly dislike, and 10 meaning: greatly love). Then there is a column where you can tally the scores. The activities that have the highest scores (rated 16 or higher) are the things both of you are mutually interested in the most. One couple that had been married for years recently took this survey and found a number of activities they didn't even know they both enjoyed!

Bonding through enjoyable activities will give you the opportunity to foster positive feelings toward each other: laughter, fun, and good memories… all the things that create romantic love.

Look-up Scriptures:
Proverbs 15:30; 17:22   Ecclesiastes 3:1-8; 4:7-11

Questions to Ask Myself:
Am I willing to spend more time doing things that both my spouse and I enjoy, even if it means I won't have as much time for my own activities? Am I willing to try new things that my spouse enjoys to see if I might like doing them, too?

Questions to Ask Each Other:
Spend your time doing the survey and talking about doing fun things together. Write down your next activity on the survey!

Prayer: Lord, help us to find a sense of joy and romance as we blend our interests. Give us an open heart and mind as we seek for mutually enjoyable activities. Fill us with a new and fresh love so that our times together are fulfilling and will revive the romantic feelings between us.

8 ☙ *I Feel Your Pain* ❧ 8

"Therefore, as God's chosen people, holy and dearly loved, clothe yourselves with compassion, kindness, humility, gentleness and patience."
Colossians 3:12

One plus one doesn't equal one – except in marriage. Psalm 133 informs us that God commands His divine blessings and presence when believers walk in unity. The same is true in marriage. One of the prerequisites to experiencing that oneness and unity is to possess a heart of compassion – a heart that empathizes with the pain of another, much like God does for us.

Many years ago, we attended a marriage seminar – not to teach or sing, but to be refreshed by being together, and learning from someone else. Unfortunately, the topic they covered the first night stirred up buried anger we had, and we almost wished we hadn't attended! We actually left feeling more miserable than before. Obviously, there were a lot of things we had to work on. And as we mentioned in the introduction, this devotional might stir up buried issues between you and your mate. Hang in there! God can give you strength to work things out. We encourage you not to quit! You'll be glad you kept up this daily devotional together.

Although we had a rough time during that seminar, it gave us some tools that help us even to this day. One of the topics they emphasized was the great human need for compassion. They explained that many of our society's psychological problems can be traced to a lack of genuine heart-felt compassion from others. In our fast-paced culture, most of us focus on ourselves – what we have to do; where we need to be – before we think of others. We could relate, just by looking at our OWN marriage. We weren't showing nearly enough compassion to each other.

Perhaps you were raised by parents that didn't display affection and were emotionally stoic and detached. Often, this will manifest itself in your own difficulty to engage on a "feeling" level, even with your own spouse. We have met some couples who find it incredibly difficult just to say, "I love you."

Like many godly characteristics and qualities we lack, we need to ask the Lord to empower and teach us to show compassion. The Bible says that God longs to show compassion to us (Isaiah

21

30:18). It rises out of His tender affection and deep love for us. Colossians 3:14 says, *"And over all these virtues put on love, which binds them all together in perfect unity."* Thayer's Greek Definitions notes that the word *"binds"* is used of ligaments which hold together various members of the human body. Compassion is a vital part of the love that "binds" us with our spouse. To be compassionate is to love… just like God does.

This concept of showing compassion is unique to Christianity. The emphasis on this trait was revolutionary in Jesus' day – and still is today. Because our nation was founded on the principles found in the Bible, this emotional characteristic was woven into the fabric of American life. And, although that cloth might be fraying – still, we are overall a more compassionate people. Even extending to other countries (where the cultural fabric is sadly moth-eaten), one can clearly see its profound effect on any nation touched by the Gospel.

Ask God for His heart of compassion for your spouse. The Lord of Love can strengthen you to fulfill this vital need we all have, especially from our marriage partner. This will greatly contribute to the unity we all want to experience in our marriages.

Look-up Scriptures:
Isaiah 30:18; 54:10; 63:7   Philippians 2:1-4
Matthew 15:32   Colossians 3:12-14
II Corinthians 1:3-4; 6:11-13   I John 3:16-18

Questions to Ask Myself:
Is it difficult for me to express compassion to my spouse? Do I take the time to show him/her empathy out of a tender affection and deep love, like God has for me?

Questions to Ask Each Other:
❦ Am I showing you the tender affection and concern you need when you encounter difficulties? ❦ Describe how I can do it more effectively?

Prayer: Lord, fill us with your compassion so we can feel what our spouse feels. Teach us to show each other empathy, as you do for us, so that our unity will increase.

"Submit to one another out of reverence for Christ." Ephesians 5:21

Recently, we heard a sermon about the curses placed on Adam and Eve because of their sin. Referring to Genesis 3:16, the speaker stated that this curse meant husbands should rule over their wives. Friends, few concepts have been as frequently distorted as God's true intentions for marriage. Because of its importance, we must always look at the whole of scripture for answers. As we do, we see balanced instructions given equally to husbands and wives and the incredible plan God had for humanity.

God's original plan was that Adam and Eve would be partners on earth and care for all of His creation together. God said it was *"not good that man should be alone"* (Genesis 2:18). God created Eve as a *"counterpart aid"* so that Adam wouldn't be alone. The Hebrew word, "Neged," means: *matching part, corresponding person,* or *counterpart.* In other words, God made the perfect match. They were "one" in every way.

Unfortunately, human nature often leads us to desire a CEO in our homes. But, this institution was created and ordained by God, and accordingly, should be run by spiritual methods, not earthly ones. God never instructs or encourages men to rule over their wives or any other woman. The "Second Adam," Jesus Christ, came to redeem mankind from the curse of sin. Because of His sacrifice on the Cross, the way was opened for couples to go back to the way things were before the Fall… just with clothes on.

While it's true that we still experience many of the effects of original sin (all women who have given birth would remind us of this), we do have an opportunity to go back to Eden; no longer struggling to dominate women as they still do in other parts of our world, which is not the attitude that Jesus demonstrated.

In our key verse above, the word, "submit," has often been misinterpreted. Thayer's Definition describes it two ways: As a Greek military term, it means, *"to arrange [troop divisions] in a military fashion under the command of a leader."* But in non-military use, it was understood to be *"a voluntary attitude of giving in, cooperating, assuming responsibility, and carrying a burden."*

Unless you are given to wearing military fatigues as a husband and wife, this latter definition probably fits you better!

The passage begins by addressing husbands and wives together in verse 21. Though, in the original Greek, it's a run-on sentence, English translators broke it into two verses. Verses 21-22 actually read, *"Submit to one another out of reverence for Christ, wives to your husbands, as unto the Lord."* Later, husbands are told to love their wives as Christ loved the Church. This would obviously involve enormous sacrifice. Both are instructed to follow Christ's example and cooperate with each other.

Imagine the joy that first couple experienced. There was complete transparency of heart and mind, no desire to break the bond they had, and no chance of breaking the other's heart. They toiled together, lived together, and loved together. Absent were the power games so many couples struggle with. Both respected the other and worked to cooperate in unity with a yielded heart.

While we do continue to fight against the devastation of sin and its affects on our marriages, we have an opportunity to achieve an idyllic oneness and unity that most couples can only dream of. And we do this by following Jesus' example.

Look-up Scriptures:
I Peter 2:21-23   Ephesians 5:21-33   John 13:14-17
Genesis 1:27-31; 2:18   Galatians 3:26-29   Matthew 18:19-20

Questions to Ask Myself:
How can I be more cooperative with my spouse? Am I willing to work together with my spouse to search for God's desires? Is my attitude following Jesus' example?

Questions to Ask Each Other:
♠ Have I given in to earthly methods, rather than spiritual ones, to stay unified with you? If so, how can I change this? ♠ Is the "Fruit of the Spirit" obvious in our relationship?

Prayer: Lord, help us to find that place of love, humility, and servanthood that You showed by Your example. Help us walk together in unity and cooperation by the power of your Holy Spirit.

"Now I want you to realize that the head of every man is Christ, and the head of the woman is man, and the head of Christ is God."
I Corinthians 11:3

When God ordained marriage He gave us a good heavenly model: Himself. God is three distinct persons in one. While the word "Trinity" is never used in scripture, the truth of the *Godhead* is found throughout the Bible; a mystery we will only fully understand in the afterlife. Denial or distortion of this truth is a critical departure from historically sound doctrine.

God the Father, Son, and Holy Spirit are our best example of perfect unity in marriage. When our key verse says that God is the "head" of Christ, it doesn't mean there is a hierarchy, or "chain of command," in the Trinity. Though Jesus voluntarily yielded to His Father's will throughout His earthly ministry, it doesn't mean the Son is in some sort of unending, one-sided submission to the Father. Throughout the Bible, we see each member of the Trinity as equal, bestowing honor on the other, giving us the ultimate model of servant-hood. They are totally unified. They are One.

Athanasius, a fourth century scholar, said of I Cor. 11:3, that the word *head* must be understood as "source" rather than "boss." To stop an early Church error, he penned the creed given his name, which said of Jesus, *"...[He was] equal to the Father as touching His Godhead, inferior to the Father as touching His Manhood."* The Father didn't rule <u>over</u> the Son. Later, Cyril of Alexandria said of our key verse: *"Thus we say that the <u>kephale</u> (which means "head" in Greek) of every man is Christ, because He was made through Him and brought forward to birth... and the <u>kephale</u> of woman is man, because she was taken from his flesh and has him as her source. Likewise, the <u>kephale</u> of Christ is God, because He is from Him according to nature."*

You might be saying, *"What does this have to do with my marriage?"* A lot. Sadly, many couples operate in a manner similar to a managerial flowchart. While it may work on some pragmatic level, and even provide a level of security for one or both spouses, there will always be something missing. As married couples, we are one flesh, and God's plan is that, like the Trinity, we work as one, honoring each other in perfect harmony. But many try to translate "head" to mean "authority/ruler." Among the problems of this view, is that it not only distorts God's relationship with Himself, but a strict application in this context would mean that all men were to rule over all women!

When the Old Testament was translated into Greek (The Septuagint), a choice was made when translating the Hebrew word for head (ro'sh). It can either mean a "ruler" OR refer to the "physical head." But when this word obviously meant "physical head" in the Old Testament, the translators chose the Greek word mentioned earlier, "kephale." It would logically follow that if the meaning of "head" in I Cor. 11 was "authority/ruler," it would be an extremely rare usage of the word. On the other hand, when translated "physical head," it would also agree with the teachings of the ancients, including the Greek philosopher, Aristotle, who believed that the man's brain was the "source/origin" of life.

Jesus is the source of life and Savior of all mankind. So, as the Son yields to the Father and promotes the Spirit, the Father commends the Son and works through the Spirit, and the Spirit always points to the Son. All give preference to the other in love, honor and perfect unity. Marriage should reflect this same attitude.

Look-up Scriptures:

Psalm 133	Ecclesiastes 4:12	Philippians 2:9
Proverbs 15:33; 30:27	Romans 12:1	II Peter 1:17

Questions to Ask Myself:
Do I honor my spouse with a willing and humble heart? Do I give preference to him/her, following the example that God gave us in the Trinity – by the way they treat each other?

Questions to Ask Each Other:
♦* Do you ever feel controlled – like I'm acting more like your "boss?" ♦*Are we operating together as "one flesh?"

Prayer: Lord, teach us to walk together in YOUR ways – not in the world's wisdom. Give us understanding so that our unity on earth will be a reflection of the unity of the Godhead.

"Finally, all of you, live in harmony with one another; be sympathetic, love as brothers, be compassionate and humble." I Peter 3:8

We once heard a teenager give a description of the man of her dreams. She said she was praying for a husband that would *"love God more than her and love her more than the rest of the world."* Talk about having your priorities right! Making the spiritual dimension top priority creates a strong marriage. But what about sorting through the rest of life, the day-to-day stuff? We think you'll agree; life can get pretty complicated. If we're not careful, we can become like unbalanced tires on a car – life will get pretty bumpy and unstable.

Bob thought he married the perfect woman. He and his wife, Cheri, loved God and wanted Him to be first in their lives. They also both agreed that their second highest priority would be each other. Their marital imbalance actually began over a much lower priority issue, not so easy to categorize: dreams and expectations. The first hint of this came when Cheri took her dream-of-a-lifetime job as the executive sales manager of a major advertising agency. This new position involved quite a bit of traveling and often took her away overnight several days a week.

Bob also had dreams. He wanted a wife that was more of a homemaker. He had always dreamed of coming home to a warm and cozy house, with a piping-hot dinner on the dining room table... just like it was when he was growing up. But Cheri was so excited about her job opportunity that she didn't take Bob's early concerns about the new position seriously. Week after week Bob sulked in silence. A deep resentment was growing in him, feeling that Cheri was more interested in her job than his desires.

Six months into Cheri's new job, they knew things were progressively getting worse. They were arguing constantly about her schedule, and to make matters worse, Bob had struck up a casual relationship with a fellow co-worker, Janice. He started staying late at work because he was lonely at home without Cheri. But, one night, when everyone else had gone home, Janice began to tell him how meaningful working with him had been. Those words sounded so good and filled his need to be appreciated. Bob knew that if he and Cheri didn't get help soon, he could easily freefall into a relationship with Janice and destroy their marriage.

When Bob and Cheri finally went for counseling, Cheri realized that she hadn't been sensitive to Bob's needs when she took her job. They weren't in agreement when she accepted the position. After a lot of talking and listening, they came up with a solution that made them both happy. She would keep the position if her firm could agree to schedule her out of town overnight only once a week. This was agreeable to Bob since it was more predictable, and Cheri was happy when her firm accepted her offer.

In our key verse, the word *"sympathetic"* in Greek means *"suffering or feeling like another"* or *"mutually commiserative."* Listening to each other's needs and responding with respect and care will help us live harmoniously together. To live in "harmony" means to be *"like-minded."* When we work toward a mutually pleasing agreement with our spouse when making our plans, we are following God's ultimate plan and will reap a peaceful and mutually fulfilling marriage. Because we are "one flesh" with our spouse, it is critical that we cooperate and communicate together until we have found the balance of common ground.

Look-up Scriptures:

John 13:35	Romans 12:10	I Peter 2:21 – 3:11
John 15:13	I Corinthians 13	I Peter 4:8

Questions to Ask Myself:
Do I listen when my spouse expresses his/her opinion about our decisions? Do I try to communicate and be understanding?

Questions to Ask Each Other:
♣ Do you feel fully informed before we come to a conclusion about a decision? Am I expressing openness and sympathy for your desires and opinions when you have a different view?

Prayer: Lord, give us sympathetic hearts that are sensitive to each other's needs and desires. Help us to develop godly habits in our communication so that we can remain unified and in love.

12 ☙ *Leave and Cleave* ❧ 12

"For this cause a man shall leave his father and his mother, and shall cleave to his wife; and they shall become one flesh." (NAS) Genesis 2:24

Years ago we knew a couple whose wedded bliss ended shortly after they got married. The husband had a close relationship with his mom, and couldn't seem to transfer loyalty to his wife after their marriage vows. Although the man was from a good Christian family, he soon found himself in the impossible state of trying to please two women, equally, at the same time. With his loyalties divided, this became a source of great pain for his wife, and a catalyst for much friction in their marriage. Thankfully, a Christian counselor was able to help this husband see the light and wisdom in placing his highest allegiance to the one he married.

In Genesis 2:24, the word "leave" in the Hebrew means to *"depart from, to let go, and to relinquish."* When we get married, this doesn't mean the end of loving or honoring our parents. Rather, we should work closely with our spouse to develop a rapport with each other's parents that is on a different level than that of a parent-child relationship. There shouldn't be a constant feeling of obligation to please them. And your spouse should know that he/she is your top priority. You are now a team. You are now one flesh.

The word "cleave" helps us understand the requirement for our new devotion and loyalty. This word in the Hebrew means *"to cling, to pursue closely, to follow hard, and to stick to."* This is a very distinctive relationship. You are no longer just two independent people making your own decisions. You are now in a relationship that God intended to be a virtuous, life-time commitment, never to be divided or weakened by others, even those that brought us in to this world. Best described by the words you've heard preachers recite in their marriage vows, *"Let no man put asunder,"* in other words, never to be separated by anyone.

When Adam first saw Eve, he said, you are now *"bone of my bones and flesh of my flesh."* Taken from Adam's rib or side, they became partners and companions. God wants your spouse to become your greatest friend and advocate. He ordained this remarkable institution for not simply the purpose of preserving mankind on the earth, but providing a lifetime partner for you.

In these verses, the Bible clearly describes the strength of the bond of marriage. When you have two people joined in the strength of that bond, and further, that have dedicated their marriage to Jesus Christ, he wraps them in a union that is stronger than any other human relationship. Ecclesiastes 4:12 says, *"A cord of three strands is not quickly broken."* God intends that your marriage be a covenant commitment between Himself, you, and your spouse... a faithful devotion to this one person that would have priority over every other relationship you have. A bond superceding even that with your parents, God has called you to leave your father and mother and cleave to your mate. If you find yourself in an emotional battle of loyalty between your spouse and another person, decide today to cling to your deepest and most important relationship... your life-long partner and friend.

Look-up Scriptures:
Genesis 2:21-25   Psalms 45:10-11   I Corinthians 11:11
Deuteronomy 5:1   Matthew 19:5   Ephesians 5:28

Questions to Ask Myself:
Am I completely loyal to my spouse, or do I battle with him/her over parental issues? Do I have a hard time deciding who to please when I can't please both my spouse and my parents? Do I "cling" to my husband/wife like I should? Have I made selfish decisions?

Questions to Ask Each Other:
💣 Do I make you feel secure in my love and loyalty? Do my actions show that you are the most important person in my life? What steps can I take to better show this? How can we work together more effectively to honor our parents without harming our loyalty to each other?

Prayer: Lord, help us to find the balance of honoring our parents while making our loyalty to each other primary. Give us listening ears to hear each other's concerns about anything that might be hurting our relationship. Strengthen us to humble ourselves to You and to each other, so we can make right decisions.

30

13 ∾   *Friendships Change*   ⤳ 13

"A friend loves at all times, and a brother is born for adversity."
Proverbs 17:17

To find true "oneness" in marriage, your spouse should always be your best friend... for life. Hopefully, this begins well before the wedding ceremony. That's what happened to us. We were best friends for over three years before we tied the knot, and we still are. This doesn't mean we don't have other friends who are very special to us. But all other relationships changed when we became one through marriage.

Fran and Sid had been married for one year when Sid's high school friend, Tony, moved back in town. Tony had recently started a business, and wanted to include Sid as a "ground level" partner in his new up-and-coming business. He convinced Sid that this was a win-win plan for both of them and that his "low-risk investment" of time and money would yield great rewards and financial benefits for him in the future. They had been buddies throughout their teen years, so Sid had no reason to distrust Tony. The only problem was: Fran didn't feel the same way.

She could read Tony. And she didn't like the book! He seemed to bring out the "worst" in her new husband. In fact, Sid started cursing again – something he hadn't done in years. Fran believed Tony had selfish motives and wanted their money to finance his new venture. Although he was always nice to her, she felt it was "sweet-talk," the kind of condescending chit-chat flight attendants hear from lecherous businessmen. She didn't trust Tony for a second.

When Fran finally got the courage to discuss her concerns with Sid, he became very defensive. He was shocked that Fran would ever think so poorly of Tony. But she stood by her feminine intuition. She also revealed her despondency at what Sid was becoming because of Tony's influence.

Fran's dislike for Tony slowly turned to disgust. But Sid continued to defend Tony, while belittling her concerns. She was soon at a breaking point, and with no change in sight, she issued an ultimatum: *"It's either me or Tony. I can't take the pressure he puts on you and how manipulated you are by all his opinions.*

You're not the man I married anymore; I want a divorce." Sid had no idea it had come to this. Fran's words rang in his head as he realized that his old friend, Tony, had become a tool to destroy the trust and loyalty between himself and Fran, his very best friend!

Sid talked Fran into seeing a marriage counselor. In those sessions, it became clear that Sid had felt obligated to Tony. He recognized that he had chosen allegiance to an old friend over his loyalty to Fran. Sid agreed to break off financial ties with Tony and spend less time with him. It was later revealed that Tony had manipulated Sid for his money, draining their savings. So, a difficult lesson was learned. Sid and Fran agreed that, from now on, they would consider each other's opinions and concerns most important, and operate as a team. They would never again let someone come between them. So God restored their love, loyalty, and trust for each other.

Friendships outside our marriage relationship, whether old or new, can become a test of our loyalty to our spouse. Making sure that we are loyal to our best and lifetime friend over all others is critical to the unity in our marriage. Not only will it help us to avoid potentially harmful situations that they may foresee more clearly, but it will protect the love of our lifetime covenant.

Look-up Scriptures:

Ruth 1:16-17	Psalm 41:9	Proverbs 20:5-6
Job 42:7-12	Proverbs 16:1-2	Jeremiah 17:9-10

Questions to Ask Myself:
Do I have any friendship that would threaten loyalty to my spouse? Am I creating the atmosphere needed to encourage unity by my loyalty, or are my loyalties divided?

Questions to Ask Each Other:
💣 Is there a friend of mine that you feel divides my loyalty to you? How can I change this to bring unity between us?

Prayer: Lord, change our hearts to care more about each other's opinions. Teach us to listen to each other's warnings so we won't step into wrong relationships. Protect us from divisive situations.

"May integrity and uprightness protect me, because my hope is in You."
Psalm 25:21

Tracy was a beautiful and talented woman. Clint was proud of his wife, as the top design artist at her advertising agency. She would usually leave for her job at noon to work a late shift. This allowed her time with their kids each morning before she drove them to preschool. Clint had them during the evenings. It was a perfect solution to their financial and child-care needs.

When Tracy and Clint decided to tackle this new schedule, they promised they'd reserve weekends for each other. They felt they could handle it until they got out of debt. But it turned out that most weekends came and went with little time for anything but grocery shopping, cleaning, laundry and a little TV. Usually, they just ended up working at home and caring for the kids.

Tracy's manager, Bob, was brilliant and caring. She constantly felt encouraged by his comments about her work. Always affirming, he would often take the first mock-up of her designs. She was flattered. One night Bob stayed late to help her with some work on one of their accounts. After a few days, he stayed late again to "complete some paperwork." But that night he didn't even push one paper across his desk. He spent the whole time talking with Tracy. She felt a little uncomfortable, but it made her feel wanted and protected.

One night, Clint called her to ask a question about their kids, and she happened to mention that Bob was there. Clint had been under the impression that she was always with Lucy, her co-worker, at night. She hastily informed him that Lucy was working in the office just across the hall. But a cold chill swept over Clint. He knew Tracy admired Bob and had felt uneasy at how often his name was coming up in their conversations. Clint insisted that she come home immediately, but Tracy was stunned at his reaction. Waiting on the porch like an angry dad whose daughter was home late from a date, he lowered the boom – insisting that she quit her job and become a full-time mom. She was devastated by Clint's harsh reaction and distrust of her character.

Although his reaction was demanding and unkind, Clint knew that Bob wasn't a Christian and had been through several relationships with live-in girlfriends. Clint read his "kindness" differently than Tracy. After Clint cooled down, he and Tracy talked things through together and each could see the other's concerns. Clint had been rash and distrusting, which really hurt Tracy, but she had been unwise to allow herself to be in a potentially compromising situation.

Tracy and Clint brought their situation to the Lord, and asked for wisdom. He directed them to revamp their schedule, so they were both happy. They realized that the stress caused by both of them working full-time simply wasn't worth it. It kept them from spending "enjoyable" time together and by the weekend, they were too tired to want to do anything. Tracy would go part-time at work, and agreed to keep a healthy distance from Bob, never again allowing herself to be alone with him in the office like before.

Building "hedges" of protection and accountability is not only wise, but critical to marriage. Even innocent relationships can sow seeds of destruction. Distance with the opposite sex promotes loyalty. And if you're not sure how much – just ask your spouse!

Look-up Scriptures:
Psalm 26:2; 32:7-10; 41:12   Proverbs 10:9; 13:6
Proverbs 2:6-11, 16-20   Proverbs 23:26-28; 27:12
Proverbs 4:5-13, 25-27   Romans 16:19

Questions to Ask Myself:
Am I willing to listen to my mate's concerns about my contact with others of the opposite sex? Am I willing to change my behavior in order to make my spouse feel more secure?

Questions to Ask Each Other:
Are there things that I can change in my behavior to make you feel more secure about my contact with others of the opposite sex? Am I acting in such a way that you feel protected?

Prayer: Lord, give us wisdom to avoid emotionally or physically foolish situations. Help us to make the choices that protect our integrity and limit the temptations that could destroy our marriage.

"Yet now I am happy, not because you were made sorry, but because your sorrow led you to repentance. For you became sorrowful as God intended."
II Corinthians 7:9

Karen felt like she had been punched in the stomach. She tried to catch her breath and make a hopeless attempt at wrapping her mind around the knightly image of Frank: the devoted husband, deacon in their church, and caring father… but the naked women on the computer hard drive said it all. The recently revealed fact that Frank was addicted to pornography was bad enough, but now, to come to the shocking realization that his lack of interest in their sex life was connected to this was unthinkable.

Karen had been longing for Frank to be more affectionate with her, but over the last few years, more and more, he just brushed her aside when she would try to hug him in the kitchen after dinner. He rarely had interest in making love any more, which seemed strange. But she simply thought he was stressed out from his job, or perhaps, had the problems that some men develop as they hit middle age and just didn't know how to talk about it.

Many men, and even some women, get snagged into soft porn that can readily be found on cable TV. But like a "gateway" drug, this often leads to hard-core pornography, which, according to neurologists, releases a chemical in the brain more addictive than cocaine.

Jesus said, if a man even looks at a woman with lust, he has committed adultery (Matthew 5:28). Pornography is lethal to a marriage and often spirals from a "fantasy" affair… into a real one. Thankfully, Frank clearly saw the devastating effects of his bondage and repented. This enabled the Holy Spirit to carry out a work of cleansing and healing in his heart. But this wasn't enough for Karen. She was humiliated and tormented.

Karen's problem was a common one. Trust is not easily regained, but when it is lost in this way… it's very difficult to get back. Neither is forgiveness easy to achieve. In a counseling session they had together, Frank apologized over and over with a true and godly sorrow. But complete healing in their marriage didn't take place until Karen began to deal with the bitterness that had attached itself to her soul. Since the revelation of Frank's problem, she had thought that the heavy cloud hanging over her was from having to deal with Frank's dishonesty. In time, God showed her that it was her own anger that was tormenting her.

As Karen asked for God's cleansing, a process of forgiveness and healing began. It didn't happen in a day. But it happened. And Frank and Karen set up guidelines under the counselor's direction to stay accountable to each other at all times. Frank also agreed to be available by phone at all times at work and at home, and to also put a porn-filter service on all computers that were accessible to him (see www.heartfortheworld.com for a link to our recommended porn-filter service). He also made himself accountable to some other men in his church. Taking these steps enabled him to find victory over his addiction.

And Karen felt a new freedom... the freedom that comes with forgiving from her heart. When she was able to forgive Frank in this way, she was released from what had tormented her soul for so long (Matthew 18:34-35). And God gave them both the strength and joy of restoring their romantic love all over again.

Look-up Scriptures:

Psalm 101:2-4   Proverbs 7:4-27   Matthew 18:21-35
Proverbs 6:20-35   Matthew 5:28-30   Galatians 6:1

Questions to Ask Myself:

Am I careful to keep my heart pure and stay away from tempting T.V. programs or internet sites? Is God pleased with my actions? Do I resist tempting thoughts when they come to mind?

Questions to Ask Each Other:

Are we doing all that we need to do to protect our marriage and family from the ungodly influences that can be found on T.V. and the internet? What practical steps can we both take to protect our emotional and physical purity more effectively? ♦What are some things I can do to help encourage your integrity?

Prayer: Lord, provide every physical and spiritual tool we need to stay pure to each other. Strengthen our hearts and minds so we'll stay loyal to You and to each other; walking in complete integrity.

"From the same mouth come {both} blessing and cursing. My brethren, these things ought not to be this way." (NAS) James 3:10

Several years ago, some friends of ours got married. They had that special spark newly married couples often have. But after a few years things had dramatically changed. The woman rarely said anything kind to her husband, and criticized him mercilessly, even in our presence. She seemed to have all the answers. Her husband sulked around like a whipped dog. It was obvious he had come to believe he was a failure. And his wife may have even agreed with his conclusion!

When this couple moved from our city, we lost track of them. It is certain that if they didn't get help, they are either now divorced or miserably married. Showing condemnation and disrespect are highly destructive – even when it's communicated non-verbally. It's easy to be caught in the trap of dishonoring our spouse by judging their actions or opinions. And like a cancer, it can destroy a relationship from the inside out.

Have you ever tried to fix your spouse's behaviors? Do you frequently think you need to "enlighten" him/her? Do you often find yourself giving advice to your spouse even when you're not asked? Do you criticize, scold, express contempt, or use other forceful methods to change you spouse? Many couples get into these controlling habits with each other, but imposing ourselves on each other this way will either lead to contentious confrontations, or depression. Our marriages should be the place where we create healthy habits that build each other up. There are certainly enough things in this world that tear us down.

All of us have come to our own opinions and actions for a reason. Sometimes it's our upbringing. We all have differing explanations for why we do the things we do. If we don't agree about something our spouse is doing or saying, we need to learn how to listen and discuss our differences and explain the reasons for our perspective. When we give each other time to share the viewpoint that guides our actions, it gives us an opportunity to persuade our spouse about our view in a way that pleases God.

Your spouse isn't crazy – ok, maybe just a little crazy, but there is a reason he/she holds to the attitudes and beliefs they have. Pray, this day, for an understanding heart and a listening ear.

Sometimes, the most loving thing to do is simply to let things go and just agree to disagree. But to criticize or show disdain is damaging behavior that can only diminish our romantic love for each other.

Sometimes it takes years of discussions to come to a real place of agreement on certain issues, but as we are open and teachable and treat our spouse's opinions with respect, we can mutually work to persuade the other without pressure or a critical spirit. James 3:17 says that when we have godly wisdom we will be considerate and submissive. As we walk together peaceably, we will reap the benefits in a deeper and growing love.

Look-up Scriptures:

Proverbs 12:1	Proverbs 21:9	James 3:3 – 4:3
Proverbs 18:13	Colossians 3:8-15	I Peter 2:22-23

Questions to Ask Myself:
Do I respect and value my spouse's opinions? How can I show respect more effectively? Am I critical or judgmental about my spouse's actions or opinions, forcing my own ideas instead?

Questions to Ask Each Other:
Do we give each other enough "listening" time to express each of our own viewpoints? What are some things I can say to you so you don't feel judged or criticized? What steps can I take to show more respect for your beliefs and actions? Give me an example of how you would like me to make a request.

Prayer: Father, please forgive us for not always presenting our opinions correctly. Forgive us for every form of criticism and every judgmental word expressed that has hurt each other. Empower us, this day, to have the same graciousness that Jesus showed. Teach us how to be respectful and thoughtful in the way we express ourselves. Teach us how to replace our judgmental and critical remarks with requests that are kind and encouraging.

*"Be kind to one another, tender-hearted, forgiving each other,
just as God in Christ also has forgiven you." (NAS) Ephesians 4:32*

A few years ago, we counseled a couple who were having sharp marital disagreements. The wife was a stay-at-home mom, overseeing the care of their two children. The problems arose each evening when the husband got home from work. As he entered the doorway of their small apartment, he would see dirty dishes piled up on the kitchen counter, dirty clothes scattered throughout... and his wife either sitting on the couch eating and watching T.V. or talking on the phone with a friend. After years of this, he almost hated coming home.

She sort of knew he didn't like her lazy habits, but she did nothing to change. After dealing with her lack of care for so long – feeling justified – he made the mistake many young husbands have made and began making demands, ordering her to change her ways. Though this appeared to work at first, as she would quickly do all he said, she often ended up in tears. His method of dominating her into changing was destroying her love for him.

She had let the house go downhill, but it went deeper – she was resentful that <u>he</u> never seemed to help her with the kids. She would make demands right back, telling him to take the kids once in a while to give her a break. But barking out commands was emotionally damaging and ultimately made things far worse. Both were wrong. And neither could realistically justify their behaviors.

Both were trying to change the other, but were using the worst possible approach: making demands. Sadly, this method will generally meet with minimal success and often spirals into a cycle of abusive behavior. There is a better way: Learning to speak with kindness, replacing commands with respectful requests, expressing our wishes gently to each other. Instead of giving orders to our spouse, we need to kindly ask them, explaining our feelings in a loving and tender-hearted way.

In Luke 6:35, we're told that God shows kindness even to the ungrateful. This is the same kindness we're told to show to each other in our key verse, Eph. 4:32. Luke exhorts that when we love our enemies and give without expectations, we are acting like children of the Most High. In other words, we're acting like God! Amazingly, it's this same kindness that leads us to repentance (see Romans 2:4). Right in line with this (and contrary to what our feelings tell us), when we are kind to our spouse, it softens their heart and makes them more willing to meet <u>our</u> desires and needs.

The operative word here is "ask" – not tell. As we learn to respectfully ask each other for the things we desire, we can grow in our love, forgiving each other, and rebuilding the damaged areas of our relationship from our improper actions. Critical to this is knowing when and where to ask. Little will be gained from late night discussions when we are already tired. But some couples find it helpful to go to a quiet restaurant or a park to talk.

By making every effort to be considerate and kind, we have a greater opportunity of getting the response we hope for. It may seem like an overwhelming mountain, but when we work to climb upwards together, we build positive experiences that create a stronger romantic love... rather than rolling back down in a snowball of needless pain. No mountain is too tall when we draw on God's love and follow the example of Jesus Christ.

Look-up Scriptures:

Exodus 34:6	Psalm 103:8	Romans 2:4
Nehemiah 9:17	Luke 6:35	I Peter 3:8

Questions to Ask Myself:
Have I been demanding of my spouse when I want something to be different? Am I willing to change my habits and learn to be more respectful of my spouse by making caring requests?

Questions to Ask Each Other:
💣 Do you perceive my requests as demands when I try to change things in our marriage? In what ways can I change my methods of asking so that it makes you feel respected?

Prayer: Lord, help us to change bad habits of ordering each other to do things when we're not happy with each other. Give us the wisdom to know how to ask in a respectful, non-forceful way.

"Get rid of all bitterness, rage and anger, brawling and slander, along with every form of malice." Ephesians 4:31

"I don't know what happens to him. It's like he's the Incredible Hulk! He just... changes." A friend of ours was describing her husband's fits of rage and anger. She knew he had taken the brunt of his own parents' tempers and even suffered some physical abuse during their angry brawls. While she could understand his behavior, in light of his childhood, it still wounded her deeply. In cyclical fashion, their children were now becoming victims of his frequent outbursts. She would valiantly defend him – but his temper was slowly destroying her. She tried counseling, but since her husband refused to go (and denied he even had a problem), it did little more than simply help her cope.

This story is played out countless times in homes all around the world. But why would anyone let <u>themselves</u> become the source of pain for the ones they love the most... their own spouse and kids? The last few days we've discussed the destroyers of marital love. These harmful behaviors can be the very seeds of these angry outbursts. When not dealt with, fertile soil is created for an emotional blow-up between a husband and wife.

For some, anger becomes a defining life issue. Like an alcoholic, these "rage-aholics" place all blame on the person that they believe made them angry. Often, they feel like THEY are the victims, and the other person <u>deserved</u> their hostility. Throwing a temper becomes a form of punishment – a type of vengeance to "get back" at the one they perceive to have hurt them. Therapists say it's a controlling method of revenge toward their spouse – a type of payback for wrongs done. Psychologists have found that people feel better after throwing tempers because they think the scale of justice has been balanced by the pain they inflict.

Amazingly, many individuals having a consistent problem with anger management can't even remember what transpires during these fits, as their adrenaline takes over. But the wounds inflicted by these tsunamis of anger are difficult to undo. This habit – almost more than any other – is an abusive behavior that destroys romantic love and must not be tolerated. In extreme cases, rebuilding constructive forms of communication will take counseling and careful supervision, especially when physical violence and abuse is involved.

Sometimes alcohol or drugs are linked to this behavior. Because it alters the personality so significantly, many counselors refuse to begin marital counseling until the underlying substance abuse problem has first been dealt with. After recovery, marriage counseling is recommended to stabilize relationship issues that might have contributed to their chemical dependency. Many marriages have been saved by these critical procedures, and after habits are reformed, romantic love can be restored once again.

If you or your spouse struggle with anger management, don't hesitate to get the counsel and assistance you need as soon as possible from someone who is trained or specializes in this area. An experienced therapist is highly recommended to help you deal with your anger through constructive and proven methods.

One of God's names is *Jehovah Rapha*, which means, the one true God who "HEALS." God is our *Redeemer* and *Savior* and He wants to restore your marriage and love for each other. He can do this if both of you are willing to submit to His will.

Look-up Scriptures:

Proverbs 15:1	Galatians 5:22-26	Colossians 3:8
Proverbs 16:32	Ephesians 4:1-2	I Peter 3:3-4

Questions to Ask Myself:
Do I lose my temper often? How frequently do I show a temper? Is it a habit? If my spouse thinks I need to, am I willing to get counseling for my anger?

Questions to Ask Each Other:
What practical steps can I take to promote peace, not anger? 💣
Do you think I have a habit of losing my temper?

Prayer: Lord, help us not to be too proud or defensive to ask for help in managing our tempers. Give us the wisdom, grace, and strength to be willing to know how to deal with destructive anger. We thank you that the cycle of anger that has come through our family line can be broken because of the Cross of Calvary.

"Above all, my brothers, do not swear-- not by heaven or by earth or by anything else. Let your 'Yes' be yes, and your 'No,' no." James 5:12

Most of us are uncomfortable with a person who seems to be trying too hard to convince us of their honesty. Like the stereotypical used-car salesman, we don't buy it when they say, *"This is a great deal... honest!"* Billy Joel was right when he sang, *"Honesty is such a lonely word."* Lying is all around us. Even Jesus was startled to meet a truly honest person. Upon meeting Nathanael in John 1:47, he said, *"Here is a true Israelite, in whom there is nothing false."*

Dishonesty is a destructive trait that kills romantic love. But it's amazing how many couples are dishonest with each other, for various reasons. Sometimes, we try to justify lying because we feel that the "truth" would only hurt our spouse. But this denies us of the intimacy that marriage affords. We need to adopt a rule of complete honesty with our spouse.

Ed and Sue had what they thought was a great marriage. She was proud of Ed's abilities and achievements. He would often arrive home late at night armed with stories of his successes that day. Although she often felt neglected, she never would have told him so. She was impressed that Ed was so smart. According to everything he told her, he was the top salesman at his office.

But cracks were beginning to appear in their relationship. When Ed would arrive home on most nights he had a similar routine: warm up supper in the microwave, sit in front of the T.V. for an hour or so, and then, up to bed... to make love to Sue. But Sue was usually not in the mood anymore. Most nights she could get out of it because she had equipped herself with a litany of excuses. But other times she reluctantly gave in.

But it wasn't good for either of them. The truth is, she was completely worn out from being a mommy all day to their three small children. She desperately needed a break, but Ed was never there to help. She just couldn't bring herself to put more pressure on Ed when he was doing so much at work. The fracture in their relationship had occurred because both Ed and Sue had been dishonest with each other. Ed wanted Sue to be proud of him, so he told little "white-lies" to make her think well of him. But at the same time, Sue didn't divulge her disappointments with Ed. She was very lonely and overwhelmed when Ed would stay at work late, night after night, but she was afraid to say anything because he'd become defensive when she asked why staying late was so important. Ed and Sue's lack of transparency were instrumental in developing deep resentments that damaged their love and romance.

One day, Sue called and found out that Ed was no longer employed. In fact, he'd been fired for his under-achievements, and was taking his days to search frantically for another job. When he was confronted, Ed finally came clean, confessing everything. What might have been a terrible thing turned out to be a blessing: Ed and Sue realized they needed to be completely honest with each other. They prayed together, as a couple, for a new job for Ed, and the Lord answered with a job that was a much better fit... and allowed him more time to be a husband and a dad. Sue also made the decision to stop bottling up her feelings, but learned to lovingly let Ed know her true feelings. As they have adopted this practice of uncompromising honesty, their love has continued to grow.

Look-up Scriptures:

Psalm 34:10-13	Proverbs 12:17	Jeremiah 23:14
Proverbs 6:16-19	Proverbs 24:26	Colossians 3:9-10

Questions to Ask Myself:
Am I uncompromisingly open and honest with my spouse in every area? Do I ever lie to avoid a problem? Do I ever lie because I think it will shield my spouse from pain? Am I willing to make myself accountable to others to learn to be honest?

Questions to Ask Each Other:
Can we make a commitment to each other to be completely honest and open about everything from now on? ✹ Have you ever felt like you need to lie to protect me? When? Are you afraid to be honest with me for fear of rejection or loss of admiration?

Prayer: Lord, give us the unconditional love for each other that you have. Convict us to tell the truth at all times so our intimacy can grow. Help us to forgive each other for our dishonesty.

20 ❧   Independence   ☙ 20

"In the Lord, however, woman is not independent of man, nor is man independent of woman." I Corinthians 11:11

There was a time when a woman was thought to be the property of a man – along with his cows and chickens. While this is still true in many places around the world; in our own country, many changes have come for women: The right to vote; new employment opportunities; and greater freedom, to list but a few. We can all be thankful for these changes. But sometimes those who felt oppressed while they were growing up will overreact later, the pendulum swinging wildly the other direction.

Mallory grew up in a strict Christian home. There was a lot of love, but many limits. Along with countless rules – bordering on a self-righteous legalism – was a firm belief that women should be "silent" and stay in the kitchen. This did not fit with Mallory's assertive and vivacious personality. She always wanted to share what she was learning and ask questions about <u>why</u> she should believe certain things. Her parents were quick to tell her it wasn't her place to question them. Her heart was crushed, and her spirit was screaming that it wasn't fair – her questions should be thought of as just as important as the boys' in their home.

As Mallory got older, she wasn't through asking questions, and she kept her determined personality through college. She ended up with a Doctorate in Psychology, and opened her own Ministerial Counseling and Family Therapy Clinic, assisting primarily the needs of ministers and their families. Her skills, along with wisdom from her Christian heritage, made her a gifted psychoanalyst and competent business leader in her community.

But when it came to Mallory's own marriage, she had some blind spots. Any time she felt that her husband, Ed, was hindering her freedom, old feelings from her strict upbringing would arise… even if it wasn't his intention to hold her back. Ed was a good father to their two sons, treasurer at their church, and also coached high-school football. He was very secure in his own identity in Christ. Like many busy couples, it was tricky balancing their many responsibilities. But Mallory wasn't always willing to discuss her schedule with Ed before making plans. She felt like he was trying to control her – arguing that she needed freedom to make decisions on her own. She wasn't interested in asking him first. As an independent, capable woman, she didn't need his "permission" to do anything.

After a while, Ed began to feel like he wasn't needed and even wondered if she would be better off without him. He even considered going to one of her therapists at the clinic, because he was becoming so resentful. Thankfully, Mallory started realizing what she was doing... and why. Her usual hardened persona morphing into an uncharacteristic softness, she apologized to Ed for disregarding his opinions. She admitted that she had been inconsiderate and demeaning – just like others had been to her during her childhood.

This was the beginning of a new phase in their marriage. Communicating with each other about decisions they made helped life flow smoothly, and also increased their romantic feelings for each other. Mallory gave up trying to prove her independence, and became lovingly interdependent with Ed. Ed finally felt needed and admired again. And God was at the center of their lives and marriage, as they learned to depend on Him together.

Look-up Scriptures:
Acts 15:2, 6   Hebrews 10:24   James 3:17
Philemon 1:14   Hebrews 12:14-15   I Peter 3:7

Questions to Ask Myself:
Do I try to work with my spouse when making decisions? Do I assume to know what my mate thinks before I ask? Is it possible that God could give direction through his/her opinions?

Questions to Ask Each Other:
What policies can we put into place to protect us from making mistakes of independent behavior? 💣 Do you ever feel left out of the decision-making process? Explain in what way. What would you have preferred me to do in those situations?

Prayer: Lord, give us the sensitivity to consider what our spouse desires before making independent decisions. Thank you for wisdom that is gained through working together as a team.

"Do nothing from selfishness or empty conceit, but with humility of mind let each of you regard one another as more important than himself."
(NAS) Philippians 2:3

Like microscopic bugs on a beautiful flower, some of the toughest things for us to communicate to our spouse are little annoyances, especially when they initially appear insignificant. But small, irritating behaviors tend to grow larger over time and can damage romantic love. This is what happened to Rachel and Lars. Annoying habits threatened their love for each other.

Lars grew up on a farm. Rachel was a city girl attracted to Lars' love for the outdoors. Growing up in a small house, she had felt cooped up most of her life and often dreamed of moving to the country. When Lars found a farm for sale two years into their marriage, she was ecstatic.

Keeping a home tidy is a challenge in a city, but even more so in a rural setting. It began to upset Rachel when Lars would fail to remove his work boots, tracking mud all over their carpet. She was also growing increasingly intolerant of his lack of personal hygiene. When Lars would come to bed smelling like the pigs he was raising, she would tell him to sleep on the couch. This became a hindrance to their sex life as Rachel often couldn't stomach the thought of making love. She was hurt by his continual lack of respect for her standards of cleanliness. The fact that he did nothing to change even made him more offensive to her.

After just a few years, Rachel and Lars' marriage was on the brink of disaster. Lars defended himself by arguing that he wasn't that dirty. He felt like she was being too picky, so he continued his behaviors. But Rachel perceived his habits as unkempt and discourteous, and therefore, it was reality for her.

Fortunately, Rachel and Lars sought the wisdom of a Christian counselor. He helped Lars to see that his wife's lack of sexual desire was directly linked to his reluctant response to taking showers at night. By changing the offensive conduct, and by respecting Rachel's desire for a clean carpet, Lars would cultivate (just like he did in their cornfield) a harvest of romantic love... and subsequent sexual intimacy. The counselor spoke in a language

Lars could understand! And as he changed his annoying behaviors, Rachel's feelings of love returned almost immediately.

Recently, we heard a pastor tell about his wife's anxiety at how aggressively he would drive when they were together. One day he tried listening to her, and simply slowed down. She was instantly happier. Out of his love for her, he decided to drive a little easier. It took the tension out of the air when they traveled... even around town. Both of them were happier for it.

It's more difficult when certain habits are imbedded deeply into our personalities or possibly have a physical cause. We may need to consult a doctor or get therapy to conquer some behaviors. We should be willing to change any habits disagreeable to our mate, whatever it takes. Even just seeking for a solution to our offensive habits can often immediately increase romantic love.

It's foolish to be stubborn about making these changes, because they only hinder our spouse's desire to be around us. If we are considerate of each other, we will work hard to overcome all unpleasant behaviors and remain the pleasing and attractive person our spouse married.

Look-up Scriptures:

Proverbs 9:9; 27:6	John 15:13	I Corinthians 16:14
Proverbs 18:1-2	Romans 12:10	Philippians 2:3-6

Questions to Ask Myself:
Can I recall any behaviors or habits that my spouse would consider annoying? Are there areas of my behavior that would encourage a deeper love in my spouse if I would be willing to change?

Questions to Ask Each Other:
♣ What three habits or behaviors would you like to see change in my life? Will you be patient with me as I try to change... to form more pleasant habits?

Prayer: Lord, We thank you for the grace you continue to show in our marriage – You know ALL our habits... and still love us. Help us to change those behaviors in our lives to become more pleasing to our mate; reflecting the love You have shown to us.

"But seek first His kingdom and His righteousness, and all these things will be given to you as well." Matthew 6:33

Walk through the "Marriage" section of your local bookstore and you'll see book after book on <u>Intimacy</u>. Most couples would admit that this is hard to achieve with the kind of stressful, complicated lives we all lead. There are pressures with raising children, managing schedules, dealing with expectations from our spouse, and juggling financial concerns. Stress can wrap itself around us like a boa constrictor and squeeze the joy out of life. How do we find the perfect balance?

Demanding times require us to step back and assess what's really important in life, and what should be top priority. We need to review our priorities in light of God's Word and make choices by what He reveals is truly important.

In our key verse, we see that God promises to provide all we need when our desire for His Kingdom is primary. <u>He</u> wants to be the answer to the following questions: What motivates us the most in life? What is our primary passion? What drives us? What do we search for most in life? The truth is that our actions will always prove what is most important to us.

The Greek word for *"seek"* is *Zeteo*. One of its meanings is *"to crave."* King David had this craving. He expressed it in Psalm 42:1, *"As the deer pants for streams of water, so my soul pants for you, oh God.* He also said in Psalm 119:97, *"Oh, how I love your law! I meditate on it all day long."* And in verse 148 of this great chapter: *"My eyes stay open through the watches of the night, that I may meditate on your promises."*

One of the most important ways that we seek God's Kingdom and righteousness is by praying and studying God's Word. When we search the scriptures and seek God <u>first</u>, blessings flow, and everything else falls into place in our lives! We will find the balance we're hoping for.

If we don't have the deep desire that David expresses, we should simply ask God to give us this longing. When you know something is God's will, you can be sure He will answer your prayer (I John 5:14-15). And we know that God wants us to seek

Him out of the love and passion we have for Him. With God as our top priority – as couples and individuals – all our other priorities will line up and make life flow the way God intends.

As you make it a priority to seek the Lord together, as well as separately, we can promise you will not be disappointed! Blessings come to those who seek the Lord. And as your intimacy with God and His Word increase, your marital intimacy will grow.

This devotional is designed to build this habit – one that you can keep for a life-time. Praying and reading God's Word together will mutually strengthen you and steer you in the right direction. Commit yourselves today to continue spending time reading and praying with each other even after this devotional is over. All of us drop the ball sometimes, so if you miss a day or two, don't give up! And be sure to seek God on your own.

God wants to be THE most important person in your life… even above your spouse! And don't forget to pray for your spouse when you get alone with God. There's great power in prayer!

Look-up Scriptures:

Deuteronomy 4:29	Psalm 9:10	Matthew 7:7-11
Joshua 1:8	Psalm 27	Hebrews 11:6
II Chronicles 7:14	Psalm 34:10	I John 5:14-15

Questions to Ask Myself:
Do I need to pray for the longing that David had to seek the Lord? How can I make plans to spend time with the Lord on my own?

Questions to Ask Each Other:
What are some ways I can plan better so that we can make praying and reading together more of a regular habit? Are there ways that we can improve our time seeking the Lord together?

Prayer: Lord, give us a heart to follow and seek You, both together and individually, in a way that isn't legalistic, but done out of passionate love for you. We ask that you would give us the longing to spend time with you and your Word. May we build a habit of walking in Your presence throughout the day. Give us a plan to seek after You. May it flow out of a heart of love and desire to know You more.

*"Whoever sows sparingly will also reap sparingly, and whoever sows
generously will also reap generously." II Corinthians 9:6*

This week we are discussing the need to review our
priorities and balance them in light of God's standards. One matter
we should evaluate is our financial giving habits. Years ago we
were offered poor advice by a well-meaning Christian accountant.
We had made a tax return mistake and owed money we couldn't
pay. *"You are giving too much to your church – that's why you're
in debt. You need to start giving on a quarterly basis so you'll
know what you have left,"* he advised. Because we couldn't see
any logical way out of our cash flow problem, and he was the
"professional," we followed his counsel. Mistake!

Up until this time we had been experiencing God's great
blessings financially. We were completely unaware that we were
giving over 18% of our income to our church and various other
ministries. But when we followed the accountant's advice, there
was never money left to give at the end of each quarter. We
weren't even able to give the 10% we felt we should. And things
didn't get any better. Until... we finally realized that God's Word
clearly revealed our wrong priorities: We weren't putting God
first, so we desperately needed to revamp our giving habits.

Malachi 3:10 says, *"Bring the whole tithe into the
storehouse, that there may be food in my house. Test me in this,
says the LORD Almighty, and see if I will not throw open the
floodgates of heaven and pour out so much blessing that you will
not have room enough for it."* God's Word teaches that there is
great blessing when we give to the Lord and consequences when
we don't. Proverbs 11:24 says, *"One man gives freely, yet gains
even more; another withholds unduly, but comes to poverty."* This
is exactly what happened to us when we held back our giving.

The principle of giving doesn't make sense to our finite
minds, but it always works. Proverbs 11:25 says, *"A generous man
will prosper; he who refreshes others will himself be refreshed."*
As soon as we returned to paying our tithe FIRST, we began
reaping blessings in many areas, including financially! Malachi
3:10 is the only time God actually asks us to "test" him. He

apparently really wants to prove Himself in this promise. And since that time, He has proven Himself to us over and over again.

Proverbs 3:9-10 says, *"Honor the LORD with your wealth, with the firstfruits of all your crops; then your barns will be filled to overflowing, and your vats will brim over with new wine."* As soon as we went back to giving our "firstfruits," God began to bless us again. As we look back, we believe that God was testing our faithfulness to him. Thankfully, we learned a lesson and changed our ways. Now, as before, we always write a tithe check for 10% immediately after making each deposit.

A righteous person is always generous (Psalm 37:26). God wants us to be generous givers, not stingy ones. He desires abundance to flow out of us so that He can abundantly bless others through us. It often comes back to us in amazing, miraculous ways. If we have faith in God and His Word, we will obey this principle. Test the Lord in this area of financial giving and watch Him bless you, too! He's waiting to bless you, your marriage, and your family if you'll put this critical principle into practice.

Look-up Scriptures:

Psalm 112	I Timothy 6:17-19
Malachi 3:7-12	Matthew 6:1-5; 23:23
II Corinthians 9:5-15	Luke 6:38; Acts 11:29-30

Questions to Ask Myself:
Am I willing to be obedient to God's Word in our giving? Do I support my spouse, so that we are free to give financially to the Lord? Are we making a high priority of this act of obedience?

Questions to Ask Each Other:
What practical steps can we take to change our giving habits? ♦*Do you trust that God will meet our needs and bless us if we give our "firstfruits" according to the promises of God's Word? Will you join me in "testing" the Lord in our giving habits?

Prayer: Lord, give us the faith we need to be obedient to your Word in the area of our finances. Fill us with the desire to be generous in every way. Bless us so that we can bless others, as we are faithful to your Word. We place our trust in You.

"The rich rule over the poor, and the borrower is servant to the lender."
Proverbs 22:7

Did you know that there are 2,350 verses about money in the Bible? Money is very important to our lives. But it is also one of the greatest points of contention among married couples today. Have you and your spouse ever disagreed about the way you spend money, save money, make money, or give your money? If you answered yes, you are in good company – most couples have had some of their most heated arguments over this issue. The question is: Did you resolve your differences?

We recently read about a couple that was finally able to come to an agreement on finances because they made a determined effort to learn more about managing their money. They worked together until they became unified in their financial decisions. But it wasn't always that way.

Joe had a misconception of a biblical principle. He thought that since he was the "head" of his wife, that he was able to make all monetary decisions by himself, without his wife's support. But his wife, Bonnie, wanted at least some involvement. And since she was working a job as well, she thought she should have a say in how they spent and saved. But Joe refused to ask or even inform her of his decisions. One day she found out that he was using all their money to buy and sell stocks. No wonder there was never extra money left for decorating or buying clothes. She had worn the same clothes for several years and they were wearing out. In Bonnie's opinion, they needed to balance their spending better, but Joe had wedged her out by not putting her name on any of their accounts. He wasn't budging, and she wasn't happy.

Finally, Bonnie decided to open her own bank account. She thought it was the only way to "teach Joe a lesson." Instead, it just made him angry, too. They were at an impasse… it was now a battle of the wills. They had both chosen to disregard each other's desires, and it threatened their marriage.

Thankfully, they both agreed to see a counselor. He tried to help Joe see that it was unreasonable to expect that he would be in complete, absolute "control" over their finances. Bonnie had some great ideas and suggestions based on her reading about financial issues and her experience in accounting. Joe realized he had been insensitive to Bonnie's desire to be involved in financial decision making, and Bonnie realized that her independent bank account didn't help them resolve the problem, but only added fuel to the fire by making Joe feel betrayed and unneeded.

At the suggestion of the counselor, Joe and Bonnie both agreed to go through a locally based Christian seminar on financial management. As they learned more about God's plans and principles, they began to see eye to eye, working in cooperation with each other, and making their financial decisions in harmony.

Look-up Scriptures:

Deuteronomy 28:1-14

Psalm 37:21

Proverbs 3:9-10

Ecclesiastes 5:19-20

Matthew 6:24-34; 22:16-21

Romans 13:7-8

Questions to Ask Myself:

Am I working cooperatively with my spouse on our finances? Am I considerate of the way my husband/wife wants to spend or save our money? Am I willing to learn more about financial planning?

Questions to Ask Each Other:

💣 Are we making wise choices regarding our spending, or are we getting into further debt? Do we need counseling or a Christian financial seminar or class? Do we seek God's kingdom first or has money or possessions become our first priority?

Prayer: Lord, help us to be wise about the way we spend and save the money you provide. Teach us how to work together so we can be unified and in harmony with each other as it relates to our financial planning. Show us where we should go to learn more about how to manage our finances and understand this area of our lives better. Thank you that everything we have comes from You.

"Come to me, all you who are weary and burdened, and I will give you rest. Take my yoke upon you and learn from me, for I am gentle and humble in heart, and you will find rest for your souls. For my yoke is easy and my burden is light." Matthew 11:28-30

It was 12 midnight when he walked in the door. Thinking of the alarm blaring in his ear again at 4:15 AM didn't thrill him, but he made himself two peanut butter sandwiches for his dinner and gulped it down with milk just like the night before. Andrew was making a name for himself at work– at both jobs. *"I may not be the smartest, but nobody's gonna outwork me,"* he mused.

Shelly had gotten used to it, barely aware of his nightly entrance into their dark bedroom. It had become a way of life. Andrew slept in on Saturdays, but was always cranky after a long, hard week. She got to sleep in on Sundays only if Andrew would take their three kids to church without her. They were tired.

When their eyes first caught a glimpse of the house they now lived in, they just knew they had to buy it! It looked so majestic on the wooded lot in the trendy new subdivision. But the questions about the wisdom of this purchase, and its accompanying stress, began almost immediately after they closed on the house. The bank had barely approved the loan when the two of them were working full-time jobs. But then Shelly went part-time at work, when their second baby was born, and then quit altogether when the third came so she could be a full-time mom. The monthly payments on their Volvo were almost over, but it was now in need of frequent repairs. Every month they went a little further in debt.

While they were well thought of in their community and enjoyed some social standing, they were no longer enjoying each other, their three small children, or their home. They had become slaves. They were now imprisoned by the many demands their choices had caused. Then, Andrew's health began to break down causing major fractures in every area of their relationship.

Wanting to be successful at a job and having a nice home and car is great... unless the stress begins to unravel your quality of life. When Andrew and Shelly became desperate for answers,

God showed up through the help of Judy and Rob, some friends at their church, who encouraged them to sell some items they didn't need to pay off their debts. They even <u>made</u> money by selling their 4 year old Volvo and getting an 8 year old mini-van that had been well maintained. Shelly began to do freelance secretarial work from her home computer for some extra money. This, along with cutting their cable T.V. service, and getting rid of a few other monthly bills, allowed Andrew to quit his second job and be a well-rested family man. They were both relieved.

This was the beginning of a more balanced routine that integrated rest for body, soul, and spirit that Shelly and Andrew desperately needed. And looking back, they realized it wasn't worth the toll it was taking on every area of their lives to keep up the lifestyle they once had. After learning about the importance of sleep, as well as healthy eating habits and regular exercise, Andrew and Shelly were feeling refreshed. They could now enjoy each other in the atmosphere of trusting and resting in the Lord. They still had some debt they were whittling away, but they were learning to make wiser choices. Saying "no" to a stressful lifestyle, and making decisions based on the principles and priorities of God's Word, gives us the peace and rest we need.

Look-up Scriptures:

Psalm 62:1	Luke 12:22-28	Hebrews 11:6
Proverbs 13:7	Hebrews 3:19-4:2	I Timothy 6:6-10

Questions to Ask Myself:
Am I resting in the Lord's ability to provide for our family? Do I trust that God will take care of us as His Word promises?

Questions to Ask Each Other:
What changes can we make to lighten our stress level? 💣*Are you willing to give up some things you want in order to create a more restful lifestyle? What things can we change that will improve our health habits in the area of sleep, as well as eating and exercise?

Prayer: Lord, forgive us for striving and worrying. Help us to trust You in every area of our lives so that we can rest. Give us wisdom to know the ways we can change to lighten our burdens.

26 ❧   Division of Labor   ᪥ 26

"All hard work brings a profit, but mere talk leads only to poverty."
Proverbs 14:23

When our boys were barely tall enough to reach over the top of the washer and dryer, we were teaching them how to do laundry. When they were even younger, they were helping do the dishes. We decided early on that if we taught them how to do everything we did, they wouldn't starve after they left home some day! It also made them much more aware of how many dishes they used, how often they put a pair of jeans in the wash, etc.

Keeping house is challenging these days. Many families have both parents working outside the home. Kids are pretty busy these days, as well. How is the "stuff" going to get done around the house? We have found that dividing household chores with everyone in the family has helped us greatly. Every marriage has a different system, but if you don't have one you are currently using, we've devised a plan you might consider...

When we speak at marriage seminars, we make fun of Barbi and her lists. She has been called a "serial" list maker! Terry used to hate making lists in the early years of our marriage... until he realized he needed them to keep up with everything in our ministry. The busier we've become, the more we appreciate lists.

Indoor and outdoor chores are a way of life for most of us. But often, it becomes a source of tension when things don't get done. Sometimes we're tempted to point fingers at each other. Here is what solved the problem for us: We made a list of chores, and then each of us put our name by the things that we "enjoyed" doing the most. Even Tyler and Travis had preferences on the list. But what about the things that no one claims? Who is really going to be excited about cleaning the toilets? We would then ask who felt strongest about getting a certain chore accomplished. If one of us was most concerned about the bushes not growing out of control, then that person clipped the bushes... and so on.

You may be asking at this point: *"What if no one cares what the house and yard look like?"* Then I guess when people visit your house, they'll know that you don't care! But at least the whole family is to blame, and no one can point at anyone else!

You're laughing. Seriously, having a "division of labor" will reduce stress in your home and teach children responsibility. Yes, children should be obedient and accomplish the chores assigned by parents, but how much better to couch it in a <u>positive</u> light and allow them some input. Keeping house is important. But it isn't the most important thing.

Tyler learned a song on his guitar awhile back that was written by Allen Levi. It was a song about two houses. One looked like a mess: bikes and toys in the driveway, dead grass from countless baseball games. Maybe it wasn't "picture perfect," but everyone in the neighborhood always felt loved and welcomed by this family. The other house was perfectly neat, but no one knew the family that lived inside. The song asks this question: Is your house just a house, or is it a home? Though cleanliness is important, our homes should be a place where God's love is felt.

In the back of this book are some sample "lists" that might be of help to you as you organize responsibilities in your family. Believe it or not, this can even be a fun thing to do, and it will help to bring order and balance to your home-life.

Look-up Scriptures:
Proverbs 6:6-11   Proverbs 21:25; 24:27   I Thess. 4:11-12
Proverbs 12:14; 14:23   Ecclesiastes 3:13   II Thess. 3:10-12

Questions to Ask Myself:
Am I willing to do my share of the chores or do I expect my spouse to take care of these things?

Questions to Ask Each Other:
Take this time to look at the chores list and discuss what you'd like to do on the list. If you plan to make copies of the list, you may want to wait to make notes on them so you can use the lists as an ongoing plan to organize responsibilities around your home.

Prayer: Lord, thank you for the opportunity to work. Help us to understand our responsibilities and never be lazy. We desire to have high standards and teach our kids a healthy work ethic by our example. May our home be a refection of the order in heaven.

"Behold, children are a gift of the LORD; the fruit of the womb is a reward. Like arrows in the hand of a warrior, so are the children of one's youth. How blessed is the man whose quiver is full of them..." (NAS) Psalm 127:3-5a

When our two sons were born, we had already been in full-time music ministry for almost three years, having traveled all over America and Europe. At one point, we had a missions trip to Romania scheduled... until Barbi found out she was pregnant and was scheduled to deliver at the time of the trip. Tyler was a bit of a "surprise" for us, but no surprise to God!

We remembered an older woman speaking to us after one of our concerts, saying, *"If something comes in the way of your trip, trust the Lord, He may have other plans."* She had the look of a seasoned prayer warrior who had spent years hearing God's voice. Her words came back to mind when we decided that it would be wiser to have the baby in Chicago, rather than Bucharest! It was God! It wasn't exactly the way we planned the timing of it, but we were thrilled to finally be starting a family.

With a new baby, we thought the Lord might settle us down; that our traveling days would be over. But "settling down" wasn't God's plan for us. He continued to bless our ministry, open up new doors for us, and shower us with the grace needed and even the joy and desire to continue in ministry.

But then Travis came along only 14 months later. Surprise number two! We finally figured out what was causing these surprises! Even with two kids in diapers the Lord gave us the grace to continue traveling. But many things did change in our lives, because having kids brings change.

When we bring children into this world, we encounter many new dynamics that affect all our relationships. There are new topics of communication, new responsibilities, and of course, new joys and memories to share. Kids are truly worth every minute of our time and effort and few would ever regret having them. They are a blessing from the Lord. But nothing affects our marriage more than having children.

This transition from being: Man+woman+sportscar, to: Man+woman+kids+dog+hamster+minivan, is a tough one for many married folks. Many couples have seen their quality and quantity of time together decrease greatly when they start having children. Much care should be given to making a priority of your relationship. The best thing we can do for each other is to protect our marriage relationship and maintain our romantic love by making "us" a top priority.

Another transition takes place when we launch our children into adulthood. Suddenly, we're no longer needed in the same way. This can be very difficult if we have found our "identity" in being a parent, having allowed our marriage to revolve primarily around our children. We need to work to keep our romance alive so that the process of letting go is a little less painful.

Deciding that we will always make our marriage of primary importance, even above our children, is also the most loving thing we can do for our kids. Getting a babysitter to watch your kids for a "date night" fills their hearts with the security of knowing that you love each other. It's a great way to model something they can look forward to in their own future. To be the best parent we can be we need to keep our romance alive!

Look-up Scriptures:
Deuteronomy 4:40; 5:29; 6:1-12   Psalms 37:25-26; 112
Joshua 24:15   Proverbs 17:6; 20:7; 31:28

Questions to Ask Myself:
Do I put our marriage above all other relationships, including our kids? Do our kids know that we love each other by our actions?

Questions to Ask Each Other:
Do we need to adjust our schedules so we can more consistently have "date" nights or time alone together? What do we need to do to make this possible: arrange a babysitter, or drop something less important from our schedule – so we can have more time together?

Prayer: Lord, we need Your wisdom to make right decisions and prioritize our lives. Help us to arrange our responsibilities in such a way that makes our marriage of primary importance. Give our kids the security of knowing in their hearts that we love each other.

"Abraham will surely become a great and powerful nation, and all nations on earth will be blessed through him. For I have chosen him, so that he will direct his children and his household after him to keep the way of the LORD by doing what is right and just, so that the LORD will bring about for Abraham what he has promised him." Genesis 18:18-19

Does this scripture reveal God's love for Abraham, or what?! And guess what? The New Testament says that if we have faith in God, we are children of Abraham and inherit the same blessings. But, now, we have a better covenant – even better than the one God made with Abraham. Parents are still responsible to direct their kids to keep the way of the Lord. But it's important, as our key verse states, that we model godly behavior *"by doing what is right"*; children always learn more by what we do than by what we say. They will copy us. A little scary, isn't it? And this goes for what they observe in our marriage as well.

We have definitely made our share of mistakes in being a good example to our boys. One time when they were real young, we were having a disagreement in the car on the way to our weekly *"family fun night."* We were traveling, and had promised our boys that this week's fun night would be a visit to *Chuck E Cheese's*. As we drove there, our disagreement became more heated. At last, one of the boys piped up from the back seat, *"Stop fighting, mom and dad."* We quickly rationalized and said, *"We're not fighting, we're just having a discussion."* They immediately countered with, *"But you don't let us discuss like that!"* And they were right.

As we sat down at the table to eat pizza, we continued our argument and soon, gave tokens to the boys to go play the games. After a few tears, we resolved our disagreement and apologized to each other. Our love was back on track. Finally, the boys showed up, coupons in hand, ready to cash them in for some toys. As we looked at the toys under the glass counter, Tyler meandered to the other end and picked out two little plastic hearts: one pink, and one blue. We were a bit puzzled about his choice that night, especially since he then gave the remaining coupons to Travis.

When we settled into our hotel, Tyler came to each of us and opened our hands, putting one of the hearts in each of our palms and folding our fingers over them. Then he pulled us together, opening our palms to each other. He was trying to say, *"Mommy, please love daddy, and Daddy, please love mommy!"* It broke our hearts. Tears welled up in our eyes as we realized that our boys hadn't seen us make up, and we had failed to apologize to them. So we stopped right there and explained that we had done the wrong thing. We said that we were sorry and that we will always love each other... and them. The joy that came over their faces said what they were too young to verbalize!

We have established four important principles since then; the building blocks for our children's security and future families: 1) Though we can't share every detail, it's good for our kids to see how God helps us through our struggles. 2) The issue isn't being perfect, but being willing to humbly apologize to each other and our kids. 3) In all things, we need to be unified, especially when making decisions about <u>them</u>. (We should go behind closed doors until we can be in agreement with each other!) 4) Reaffirming our lifetime commitment gives our kids security, and it seals our vow in our own hearts... there is no turning back from this covenant!

Look-up Scriptures:

Malachi 4:6	Mark 10:13-16	Ephesians 6:2-4
Mark 9:37, 42	Galatians 3:6-9	James 2:21-23

Questions to Ask Myself:

Do I realize that the way I act in my marriage is affecting the patterns my kids are learning for their future marriage? Will I do whatever is necessary to be a good role model for them to follow?

Questions to Ask Each Other:

Do we apologize to our kids when we make mistakes? Are our kids seeing us as unified in decisions relating to them so that they can respect our marriage and our authority?

Prayer: Lord, teach us how to live a more consistent Christian life in front of our kids so that they have a godly example to follow. Help us to be willing to apologize; may they see a unified mommy and daddy. Give us wisdom to communicate the things that will bless them for a lifetime in their own families someday.

"Let him kiss me with the kisses of his mouth-- for your love is more delightful than wine." Song of Solomon 1:2

All of us have needs that, if ignored, leave us emotionally, physically, or spiritually starved. Not being aware of our mate's needs can siphon off, and even empty, the romantic love from their heart. All of us have a God-given need for love. Psychologists and counselors have referred to this need as a: *"love tank," "love cup,"* or *"love bank."* These word pictures illustrate that each of us have needs that, when filled by our spouse, satisfy us, but like a dry and parched desert, if our needs are not cared for or nurtured, all our feelings of love can be drained out, leaving us love-thirsty and dried up. Understanding each other's needs is critical to filling up and maintaining our romantic "love tanks."

In our key verse, this lover shares a common longing of wives. For most women, the act of sex is just the *"icing on the cake,"* whereas for a man, it's the *"main event."* Women are like slow cookers. It takes them longer to warm up and longer to cool down. If a wife feels like she can't kiss her husband without him getting aroused, she won't be as inclined to respond to his gestures of love because she feels used. Non-sexual affection is the steady, moment by moment atmosphere that makes her feel loved. And when that need is fulfilled, she is more easily drawn by a desire for sexual encounters with her husband.

Not to be crass, but most men could make love watching the news at the same time, because it's such a strong physical urge. But a woman is drawn by every move, sound, and smell that she encounters throughout the day. When she wakes up, she wants to be kissed by her husband, without assuming it will lead to sexual intercourse. She wants to be hugged in the kitchen before work. She wants a phone call from her caring husband asking about her day and how she's doing. And when they get home, she wants another hug and a loving kiss, and to be held and told how pretty she is. (Men, consider reading *"Tips for the Romantic Man"* in the back of this book. Try it... you'll like it! And so will she!)

Wives want their husbands to gently touch them and hold them; morning, noon, and night. It's an affectionate environment that makes her feel like opening up to her man. It is as vital as eating and sleeping to her "love cup." It communicates security, love, protection, comfort, and approval. And sends a message: *"I want to take care of you, protect you, and keep you safe. You are the most important person in the world to me. I'm so proud you're my wife and am concerned with everything about you."*

A tender touch or a firm hug is what she needs, guys, not just once, but many times a day. And don't forget the love notes, flowers, an unplanned dinner out, a surprise visit to her job in time for lunch, holding hands, walks in the park, a back rub... Whew! There are <u>so</u> many ways to say, *"I love you so deeply."* These gestures of love help a wife to connect to her man emotionally and physically. Without them, she feels distant, alienated, and starved for attention.

Though often difficult for a husband to understand, most of his wife's affection isn't meant to be sexual. In fact, she may find it near impossible to want sex until her needs for affection are fulfilled. Husbands, it is a choice to nurture romantic love and to cherish your wife in the way that she needs most.

NOTE: If a person has been sexually abused, and sexual issues are irresolvable, it is recommended that one contact a professional Christian therapist, specializing in this area.

Look-up Scriptures:
Song of Solomon 1:3, 13-14   Song of Solomon 8:1, 3, 5
Song of Solomon 2:6; 3:6; 5:3-5   Luke 6:31

Questions to Ask Myself (Husband):
Have I been aware that my wife has a deep need for affection? Am I willing to work at changing my daily and even my moment by moment habits to better meet this need? What can I do to start?

Questions to Ask Your Wife:
Will you forgive me for sometimes not giving you the affection you desire and need? ♠*Explain ways I can fulfill your needs for affection? Describe, step by step, what you want me to do.

Prayer: Lord, enable us to understand each other's needs. Help us to build good habits that will last a lifetime and satisfy our spouse. Remind us to put into practice the things we have learned.

"I slept but my heart was awake. Listen! My lover is knocking: "Open to me, my sister, my darling, my dove, my flawless one. My head is drenched with dew, my hair with the dampness of the night." Song of Solomon 5:2

In the same way that men rarely comprehend their wife's need for an affectionate environment, wives rarely understand their husband's need for sex. God created men to have an innately strong sexual drive. A wife may think that her husband is overly needy in this area. She might even occasionally feel that she is just a sexual object to him if she doesn't understand this inborn need.

Many married men believe their sex drive is unusually strong, and some even wish they could tame down their desires. But husbands and wives need to know that God made men this way, and a wife is in a unique place to fulfill this need.

Statistics show that close to 50% of married couples have had to endure the heartache of an extra-marital affair. Perhaps, one of the reasons for this is the lack of premarital training to gain understanding of the sexual needs and differences between men and women. Most couples enter marriage with misconceptions of what to expect out of their physical relationship.

Men often feel cheated when their wives don't have the same intensity of desire for sex that they have. A man commits himself to one woman, to remain faithful until death, trusting she will meet his sexual needs. But if, after a few years into their marriage, she becomes indifferent to love-making, he will either fulfill his needs elsewhere or, if he's a moral man, will remain very frustrated. A couple's physical relationship is a good barometer for the health of their marriage. Like falling dominos, if they are not meeting each other's physical needs, other areas will fall down. Both must learn to understand and nurture each other's physical needs to maintain their romantic love for each other.

Though many women enjoy sexual intercourse, their natural desires don't drive them in the same way as men. Most women have to learn about their own sexuality to completely enjoy it at the same intensity as a man. But most men don't just want their wives to offer their bodies to them; this isn't what fulfills them the most. A husband is most satisfied when he and his wife can both enjoy the sexual experience. Most men would agree that a wife simply "servicing" them is significantly lacking. In the back of this devotional are references to books that give practical guidelines for encouraging areas of sexual development. Learning useful steps to sexual fulfillment will help a husband and wife to become sexually compatible and satisfied. This takes sensitivity, time, and prayer. God created you to enjoy each other this way.

As our key verse makes clear, God understands sexuality and romance. He wouldn't have given major coverage to this area in a whole book of the Bible if fulfillment in romance and your sexuality were not important to Him. He wants to bless you, even in your physical relationship and fulfillment.

The first thing we did when we entered our hotel room on our wedding night was to kneel and pray. We dedicated our sexual intimacy and covenant commitment to God and asked Him to bless us as we honor Him. Over the years, God has been faithful to teach us many things as we seek Him. No one cares more about your sex life than your Creator and heavenly Father.

Look-up Scriptures:
Song of Solomon 1:10; 2:10   I Corinthians 7:3-6
Song of Solomon 3:4; 4:1-9   Proverbs 5:15-23

Questions to Ask Myself (Wife):
Have I realized how deep my husband's need is for sex? How can I become more compatible with my husband sexually? How can I explore new ways to enjoy love-making so that we both desire it?

Questions to Ask Your Husband:
In what ways can we learn how to satisfy each other's physical needs: books, counseling, discussing our desires? Are you interested in exploring new ways with me to fulfill these needs? What are some practical steps I can take to start this process?

Prayer: Lord, show us the things we can do to become more sexually compatible. You created sexuality, and want us to enjoy this area of our marriage. Show us ways we can change and help us to learn to do the things that satisfy each other. May we both know the pleasures of mutually satisfying love-making.

"My dove in the clefts of the rock, in the hiding places on the mountainside, show me your face, let me hear your voice; for your voice is sweet, and your face is lovely." Song of Solomon 2:14

Question: Who was your best friend two months before you got married? Most people would name the person they married. If you were like most of us, you spent hours and hours talking and doing things together. Even important things like term papers, job related responsibilities, etc., were all put on hold just so you could be with the one you loved the most. Sometimes you would just meet to talk and be with each other.

Marriage often swallows up time for quality conversation and activities – the very things that helped draw us together. *"Why won't he talk to me anymore?"* a wife might say. On the other hand, the husband might think, *"Why doesn't she like doing the things we used to do together?"*

A woman has a profound need to talk (the men are smiling). Men want a playmate to do things with. Common interests and time spent talking together drew us like a magnet before we were married. But interests can change and we can grow apart from our best friend. Some counselors may claim that this is okay, but most will confirm that this is a recipe for disaster. To nurture a healthy relationship, we have to spend time together in meaningful conversation as well as doing things that we mutually enjoy. You really <u>can</u> be best friends again.

If a couple is growing apart because their lives are going in different directions, efforts must be made to re-establish mutual interests. Marriage therapists recommend that a minimum of fifteen hours of *"undivided attention"* be given to each other every week. This means that watching a movie, which distracts our attention, or having dinner together while on the phone with your boss, doesn't count. Some men may say, *"I couldn't possibly come up with that many hours in a week to give her my undivided attention."* But a counselor would say, *"You came up with more than that when you were dating!"* It still takes quantity as well as quality time to maintain romantic love, and even more to revive it.

Sometimes a couple stops spending time together simply because of job responsibilities. But, because of its importance, if finances interfere, then priorities need to be rearranged.

On the other hand, a husband might lose interest and avoid conversations with his wife if he feels manipulated, or if only more demands are placed on him. Our conversations can even become destructive if they turn into a means of punishing our spouse for past mistakes. When we give each other *undivided attention,* our discussions should be considerate and sensitive. We should learn to care about each other's interests so that the topics of our conversations are mutually interesting. Women fall in love and stay in love with men who take time to talk and understand them.

In the *Blessings of Bonding* devotional that you read in the first week of this book, we emphasized the importance of spending time doing mutually enjoyable recreational activities. These can be combined with the fifteen hours of *undivided attention* only if they allow you to engage in meaningful conversation at the same time. Watching football while talking to each other, doesn't count. (Sorry guys!) Spending quality and quantity time in conversation and mutually enjoyable activities nurtures your romantic love.

Look-up Scriptures:
Proverbs 10:19   Proverbs 14:1   Proverbs 18:2
Proverbs 11:12-13   Proverbs 17:22   Ecclesiastes 3:1-8

Questions to Ask Myself:
Do I give enough time to conversation and recreation to build up my marriage relationship? Am I willing to lay aside my own desires to devote the time needed to strengthen our romance?

Questions to Ask Each Other:
Are we spending enough time giving each other our undivided attention? ✦Do you feel that I need to adjust my priorities to give our relationship more conversational and recreational time?

Prayer: Lord, teach us ways that we can bless each other during our times of undivided attention. Give us special times of bonding and romance so that we can revive the love that drew us together.

32 ❧ Physical and Domestic Care ❧ 32

"She watches over the affairs of her household and does not eat the bread of idleness. Her children arise and call her blessed; her husband also, and he praises her." Proverbs 31:27-28

While women respond to affection: a hug, a kiss, or a loving touch; men are generally more visually oriented. Most women could see a naked man and not get too excited if there isn't a relationship attached. But men are different. Husbands need wives to take care of their bodies and their homes.

Regarding physical care, we're not talking about trying to be a beauty queen. But sometimes the pressures of life can hinder us from remaining the attractive person our husbands married. Some may think it's superficial to emphasize appearance, but the point here isn't how attractive you are to the public, it's how attractive you are to the man you married. A wife should love her husband enough to care what <u>he</u> thinks of her appearance.

Areas of discussion with our husband could include: weight control, use of makeup, clothing, finding a pleasing hairstyle, and personal hygiene. It's important for a man to be sensitive and willing to support his wife in her efforts to re-evaluate her physical needs. But it should never become a cause of self-condemnation for any wife who might struggle with these issues. The fact that she <u>tries</u> speaks volumes to her husband. Our love should compel us to do everything possible to be attractive to him. Of course, there are situations where this is simply not possible because of illness, hereditary issues, etc. Further, the Bible makes it clear that inner character is top priority. But, taking care of our appearance meets an important need every husband has.

So, do husbands get a free ride? No. For some women, issues of weight, personal hygiene, hair, clothing, etc., may be very important, but usually less so. Men, ask your wife how she feels.

Concerning domestic care, many women are working and can't be the sole caretaker of household responsibilities. But most men have a deep need for their wives to care about the overall atmosphere in their homes. Men want a place to go where they find peace and rest. Women tend to have more of a capacity to create that environment. They are often more keenly aware of smells, sounds, and cleanliness. (And guys, that's why candles and romantic music are important to your wife when you are creating an atmosphere for love-making. Watching baseball on TV may hinder the "mood" for what could've been a special time.)

When a woman oversees the care of her home environment, it becomes a peaceful place for her husband to come home to. You may say, *"But I work as much or more than my husband, should I be responsible to do everything?"* No. Thankfully, many men are taking up the slack in childcare and housecleaning. But there are still many men who think that childcare and cleaning is a woman's domain and that they are doing a favor to help their wives.

In the fourth week of this devotional we discussed the *Division of Labor* regarding chores. When choosing the chores, you may have come to a stalemate on who does the left over ones – those neither of you want to do. When no one takes responsibility, our homes can become uncomfortable and be a nagging reminder of more work. This is an opportunity to make deposits in our spouse's "love bank." Men, if you know it will make your wife happy, why not push the vacuum cleaner around? Women find a man with a vacuum cleaner quite sexy! Endeavoring to please each other in these practical ways will nurture romantic love.

Look-up Scriptures:

Proverbs 31:10-31   Song of Solomon 7:1-7
Song of Solomon 6:5-10   Song of Solomon 8:10

Questions to Ask Myself (Wife):
Do I care enough about my appearance and our home? Am I willing to make changes he desires out of my love for him?

Questions to Ask Your Husband:
Will you encourage me as I learn to fulfill your needs for my physical and domestic care? ●*Describe things you wish were different about our home environment? ●*What are some practical steps I can take to become more attractive to you?

Prayer: Lord, help us to be sensitive to the areas that mean the most to each other. Give us willing hearts to change so that our romantic love for each other will increase.

"Like a bird that strays from its nest is a man who strays from his home."
Proverbs 27:8

Gloria married Tim after only 6 months of dating. She was swept off her feet by this tall, dark, and handsome man. He was everything she had hoped for. An auto mechanic for a car dealer in town, he had that rugged, yet sophisticated demeanor that made her feel protected and secure.

After 4 years, they had had two babies and were well on their way to having the large family she always dreamed of. All she wanted was to be a wife and mother and raise a happy family. All this came crashing in on her when Tim lost his job. Up until then, he seemed to be doing great. But what she didn't know was that Tim had been slacking off at work. She had perceived him to be a hardworking man, never realizing that he had been warned frequently about losing his job if he didn't put more effort into his work. Now they were left with the sudden challenge of finding another stable job for Tim to pay their mounting bills.

It took several years for Tim to land steady work to meet his family's needs, and it was a trying time for their marriage. But many lessons were learned through this unstable period. These days, many women choose to work jobs in or outside of the home, taking on some of the financial responsibilities, but few would want the sole burden for this task, and many women still expect their husbands to bear the primary responsibility as bread-winner. When a man doesn't fulfill his financial obligations, it causes his wife to feel insecure and unloved.

Women need security. The best thing a man can do for his wife is make her feel secure in his commitment, honesty, and care for her and their family. And this isn't just in the area of financial support. When a wife becomes a mom, her kids become a critical extension of who she is and how she feels. If her children aren't happy, she's not happy. If they are sick, she feels terrible. In fact, if she can hear them whimpering from another room, it's difficult for her to think about having a romantic night with her husband. She is deeply, emotionally attached to her children, so everything about her kids makes an impact on her.

If a husband neglects spending time with his kids, she bears the pain of this absence, because she often better understands her kids' vital needs in this area. The same is true with discipline of the children. If the wife feels like she is alone in this, and that her husband isn't fulfilling his role as a father, it will dishearten her.

A woman needs a strong family unit where she feels the support of her husband's parenting in every aspect. She needs him to father their children with consistent, loving, and informed discipline as well as attention. Because college doesn't teach us how to raise children, we as parents need to make efforts to learn more about parenting, just like we learn about marriage. Good parenting takes quality and quantity time and a teachable spirit.

Sometimes men can feel overwhelmed with all the roles they must fulfill in marriage and parenting. Some may retreat to avoid failure. But a marriage is highly affected by this commitment to fathering. When we take our family commitment and support seriously, our wives will feel secure and happy. You will be well on your way to nurturing romantic love.

Look-up Scriptures:

Psalms 128   Luke 1:13-17   Ephesians 6:4
Malachi 4:6   Luke 11:9-13   Colossians 3:21

Questions to Ask Myself (Husband):
Am I willing to learn how to be a better father and support my family more? In what ways do I need to change?

Questions to Ask Your Wife:
Will you encourage me as I learn to become a better father and support to our family? ☀ What are practical ways I can change, in my schedule and habits, to be what our kids need me to be? What would you like to see change in the ways I support our family financially?

Prayer: Lord, give us patience to grow together. Give us the wisdom we need to support and encourage each other in the areas of parenting and finances. Reveal the ways that we can change to satisfy our spouse's desires and revive our romantic love.

"I have been crucified with Christ and I no longer live, but Christ lives in me. The life I live in the body, I live by faith in the Son of God, who loved me and gave himself for me." Galatians 2:20

When we become a Christian, we should no longer depend on our own strength to get through life. Day by day we learn to have faith in God and find our security and significance in Him. As we do, we can cultivate the romantic love in our marriage by ministering to our spouse in God's power.

In Philippians 4:12, the apostle Paul said, *"I know what it is to be in need, and I know what it is to have plenty. I have learned the secret of being content in any and every situation, whether well fed or hungry, whether living in plenty or in want."* We may not have come to the place yet where we can say we are content in every situation. But as we trust in the Lord, His Spirit fills us and gives us power to be what God's Word and this devotional study book encourages us to be.

We encountered difficulty in our own marriage when we tried to find security in each other. We had both been saved at an early age and had attended Bible College together, but we still hadn't learned to make the Lord our ultimate foundation. It didn't take too many months into married life for us to realize that we didn't love each other perfectly or unconditionally. And we certainly weren't always able to live up to the "Mr. and Mrs. Wonderful" we both thought we married. That's when God began to teach us how to rely more on Him. When our security was shaken, we turned to God. Once we did this, we were in a much better position to minister to each other's needs.

Statistics reveal that even when a couple has a very good marriage, strenuous trials can shake the foundation of their love and commitment to each other. Serious traumas can be especially trying. When a couple goes through a severe accident, a tragic loss of a loved one, a life-altering illness, or any number of devastating experiences, you will often hear of an ensuing separation or divorce. This happens because the foundation of our life is tested at these times. If we are not firmly planted in God's Word (depending on His life and strength in us) we won't weather the storms of life nearly as well. But when we make God and the truths of His Word our foundation, we cannot be shaken off course.

There are countless stories of couples that have weathered the worst of life's storms and come through unwavering and even able to reach out to encourage others. If we place our trust in ourselves or our spouse, it can cause us to attempt to control them or manipulate circumstances. This is a dark, lonely road that leads to one place: fear. This all-consuming fear comes in many forms: fear of our spouse's failures, fear of what others think, fear of rejection, etc. But, peace and contentment come when we understand God's deep love and kindness toward us, and trust that He will provide for us, in spite of the failures of others... even the failures of our own spouse. And as we trust in the Lord, HE gives us the power to love our spouse in their deepest areas of need.

Finding our security in God's love empowers us to accept our husband or wife unconditionally. It's then that we can minister to their needs, even when they fail us. This is a foundation strong enough to last for a lifetime.

Look-up Scriptures:
Proverbs 3:25-26; 29:25   Philippians 1:20-21; 4:12-14
Luke 6:49; 12:4-7   James 1:2-4; I Peter 3:14-15
John 15:5-6; Romans 8:15   James 1:12; I John 4:15-21

Questions to Ask Myself:
Who do I really depend on? Have I found my security in God or am I looking too much to my spouse? Do I trust God in trials?

Questions to Ask Each Other:
How can we both trust God and rely on Him more? How can I minister to your needs better? ☀ Do you feel like I try to control our circumstances out of fear? In what ways am I doing this?

Prayer: Lord, give us the strength and understanding to rely on you more. Teach us and counsel us by your Holy Spirit how to depend on your love so that we can, in turn, love each other with that same unconditional love. Teach us how to minister to each other as we continue to seek you and find answers in your Word.

"Salvation is found in no one else, for there is no other name under heaven given to men by which we must be saved." Acts 4:12

You have noticed that throughout this devotional we have talked about the need to be unified with your spouse. There is one area where this is most critical and provides a foundation for all other areas: The need to be unified spiritually.

God has shown His love for mankind in manifold ways. He began speaking thousands of years ago, long before there was a written language. The Bible tells us that *"The heavens declare the glory of God."* Anyone can look at the sky at night and intuitively know that there is a Creator. The odds of this universe "just happening" by some mere chance are beyond the borders of logic.

Beating inside each human being is a heart that longs to know they were placed here for a <u>purpose</u>. Even the atheist has this longing. One day, the famous artist, Picasso, a lifelong atheist and adulterer, grabbed the hand of the only woman he ever really loved, and hurriedly brought her to a local chapel. Incredulous, she cried, *"You don't even believe in God!"* Picasso responded with, *"I know, but there just <u>might</u> be something here!"*

He could feel it!

God created us so that He could have a relationship with us. But as you'll recall, Adam and Eve disobeyed God, were banished from the Garden of Eden, and the propensity to sin entered the human race. But, sin causes separation from God, because He is holy and will not abide in sin's presence. But, He had a plan...

The Bible says we <u>all</u> have sinned. Although we may not have broken all of the 10 Commandments, we've broken at least some of them. *"But I've never cheated on my wife,"* you might say. Jesus said, if you <u>look</u> at a woman in lust, you commit adultery in your heart. God has a count of every wayward look and lie. Our best efforts aren't good enough to enter His presence.

Jesus Christ, who was God in the flesh, paid the penalty for our sin; a debt we could never repay. He was sinless and gave Himself willingly on the Cross; dying a horrible death. Placed in a borrowed tomb, He arose three days later showing Himself to hundreds of witnesses. While some may try to diminish His impact, even those who would marginalize Jesus would have to admit that *Jesus' life changed everything!* Much of Western Civilization owes its existence to this tender-hearted man who forgave the adulterer, wept when people died, and loved children.

But simply knowing this story isn't good enough. To establish a relationship with God there must be repentance. This means you have to *"change your way of thinking"* about who you are (your need) and who Jesus is (your Savior). Repentance is simply turning from your own way and turning God's way.

For the person who is already a believer, the power to live the Christian life comes from being filled with the Holy Spirit. Ephesians 5:18 says, *"Do not get drunk on wine... Instead, be filled with the Spirit."* This day by day, moment by moment power is available to you right now. The Holy Spirit will empower you, even when you've lost your own strength, and He will give you the ability to nurture your relationship and have a better marriage.

Look-up Scriptures:

Mark 8:34-37

John 20:22

Acts 2:38; 3:19; 4:31

Romans 1:16-17; 3:10

Romans 3:23; 5:8; 6:23; 10:9-10

Ephesians 2:8-9; 3:16-21

Questions to Ask Each Other: Have you ever asked Jesus to be your Savior? Will you pause right now and say the prayer below? If you are already a believer, would you ask Him to fill you with the Holy Spirit so that you can live effectively for Him?

Prayer: Dear Jesus, I acknowledge that I am a sinner in need of a Savior. I confess that I have broken your law. I place my trust in your death on the Cross and your resurrection, which has paid the penalty for my sins. I now choose to turn from my old way of life and turn to you. Please help me to live for you. Amen

Note: If you prayed this prayer, we encourage you to share your decision with your spouse. We also encourage you to contact a pastor and get involved in a Bible-believing church. We have some free materials we would love to send to you. You can contact us at www.HeartForTheWorld.com. God bless you!

"He created them male and female and blessed them. And when they were created, he called them 'man'." Genesis 5:2

Our key verse above is very interesting in the King James Version. It reads, *"Male and female created he them; and blessed them and called their name 'Adam' in the day when they were created."* *Adam* is used for <u>both</u> Adam and Eve. In the Hebrew, this word means, *"mankind,"* or *"human being,"* signifying *"red earth."* It was a humble reminder to both of where they originated from. The first <u>male</u> human, named *Adam*, and his beloved <u>female</u> "adam", named *Eve*, were unique. Distinct from the animal world, they were the beginning of the human race God had created.

Though public schools today teach that human beings evolved from *apes*, there are numerous missing links of evidence to prove the connection. Advocates for this viewpoint are still hoping for discoveries that will provide clear documentation of a common DNA and fossil ancestry, connecting mankind to animals. One thing is for sure: there's a big difference between humans and animals. The Bible teaches that we are uniquely created with a soul; and, unlike animals, can fellowship with God.

God did an amazing thing. He decided He wanted <u>two</u> variations of "adams." This was not a politically correct, gender-neutral Adam, either. He created them male and female; giving mankind unique abilities for companionship, partnership, and procreation with someone that is similar, yet practically the opposite at the same time. But, often, husbands and wives are so different that they get really frustrated because they just can't comprehend the opposite sex. Like the popular book describes, *"Men are from Mars, Women are from Venus."*

Wives will say one thing, but their husbands hear another thing altogether! Ladies, have you ever been explaining something to your husband and half way through you see a glazed look in his eyes and can tell he isn't getting it? If he's still listening he says, *"What does that have to do with what you were saying before?"* Totally exasperated, you say, *"EVERYTHING!"*

Men and women think differently. Imagine lots of small boxes and you'll catch a vision of the male mind. Men compartmentalize life: wife, kids, finances, house, car repairs, job, etc. If you try to mix these, like women do, it confuses men. Women fill those small boxes, too, but unlike men, they'll dump them all out into one box, so that everything relates to everything else. This is why women sometimes will intuitively see an outcome far in advance of when it occurs. But it also allows men to overcome emotionally charged situations quickly. A man can reprimand another man on the job, and soon, both of them are laughing and discussing their golf games! Put two women in this situation and things won't change as fast.

We're also different socially. As our friends, Bob and Yvonne Turnbull say, women love to talk... even in the bathroom. We talk all the way there – while we're in there – and all the way back, resolving all the world's problems in between. Can you imagine a man asking another man to go to the bathroom? *"Hey Tom, I'm going to the men's room. Would you like to go with me?"*

And then there's *temperature*, and *asking for directions*, and how about the *25,000 words* women say in only one little day compared to just *10,000* that come out of a man's mouth. By the time we cover all the differences between Tarzan and Jane, *we find that we're REAL different!* But these two very diverse *Adams* can have lots of fun together if they learn to understand their differences!

Look-up Scriptures:
Genesis 1:27-28   Galatians 3:26-29
Romans 1:25   II Thessalonians 2:10-12

Questions to Ask Myself:
Beyond the physical differences, have I seen how very different my spouse is from me? Am I willing to learn more about those differences and be more understanding?

Questions to Ask Each Other:
Have you seen this difference in "thinking patterns" displayed in our marriage? Are you willing to work with me to be more understanding of our differences?

Prayer: Lord, thank you that we are both so different! Thank you that our differences can be used to make us wiser and stronger.

"Then Peter stood up with the Eleven, raised his voice and addressed the crowd: 'Fellow Jews and all of you who live in Jerusalem, let me explain this to you; listen carefully to what I say'." Acts 2:14

God has designed many different personalities for mankind. Some, like Peter, have this ability to light up any room they walk into. They are the extroverts; always quick-witted, always telling stories, and always hanging around other people. Understanding our mate's personality gives us insight so we can better appreciate and learn from each other's differences.

Like indelible ink, before we are even born, we are each stamped with characteristics unique to who we are. Psalms 139:13 says, *"For you created my inmost being; you knit me together in my mother's womb."* God knew and formed us individually and personally before birth. In fact, He told the prophet, Jeremiah, *"Before I formed you in the womb I knew you, before you were born I set you apart; I appointed you as a prophet to the nations."* Likewise, God knew all about you even <u>before</u> he formed you!

Your spouse has been given a unique personality, too. It was one of the things that drew you to him/her in the first place. But, the personality you loved <u>before</u> marriage may be what you have had to *adapt* to <u>after</u> marriage. There are strengths and weaknesses in all aspects of every personality.

Justin and Megan were complete opposites. They had met in the parking lot of the University. Megan's car had broken down and Justin happened to walk by. Quiet and modest, he felt most content fixing things. And as a computer science major, he could program a computer <u>or</u> fix a broken heater hose on a car. Although he never said much, Megan felt secure when they were together. He was the strong, steady, silent type. But Megan also loved being with people; laughing, talking, and having a good time. She had that kind of bubbly personality that people love.

They married right after college and settled into a small house near the technical college where Justin was doing his post-graduate work. Soon a pattern was clear: Justin would spend hours at the computer or pouring over technical manuals. Often he would go days without even leaving the house. This was driving

Megan crazy. She wanted to go out to eat, walk around the mall, or get together with some friends. But she wanted to do it with Justin. Two very different personalities were colliding.

On Wednesday night, their church was giving personality tests for couples. Knowing that Justin loved analytical things and was used to tests, Megan talked him into going. The test revealed numerous things that helped them understand each other's needs. So, Justin dashed off to get an organizer, and true to form, marked down every Friday night for the next two months for a date night or a social get-together with friends. Justin was just beginning to see what made Megan tick. And Megan was realizing why Justin needed peace and quiet, so she gladly gave him the time and space to delve into his books. They were two very distinct personalities and were learning to appreciate each other more.

Psalm 139:14 says, *"I am fearfully and wonderfully made."* We all are wonderfully made by God! As we learn more about each other, we can actually gain strengths our spouse has. As we grow in understanding and respect for the other's personality, our differences can become a blessing, not a burden.

Look-up Scriptures:
Genesis 5:1   Psalms 139:13-16   Isaiah 40:26-31
Psalm 104:30   Song of Solomon 6:9   Isaiah 42:5-10; 45:18

Questions to Ask Myself:
Has my spouse had to "adapt" to my personality? Are there things I could modify to make him/her happier?

Questions to Ask Each Other:
What are some of the differences you see in our personalities? Are there some practical ways we could adapt better to each other? What would it look like? Do we appreciate our differences?

Prayer: Lord, we thank You that our personalities are a part of who You have made us to be. Help us to adapt to our mate in a way that makes life more fulfilling and enjoyable for them. Thank you that you have placed us together. Revive and restore the spark that originally brought us together.

"Now about spiritual gifts, brothers, I do not want you to be ignorant."
I Corinthians 12:1

When we first got married, we were so different from each other in so many ways. Neither of us had ever studied about differences in genders, personalities, or spiritual gifts and how they can affect a marriage. We just knew we loved each other very much and wanted to spend our lives in ministry together. Over time, spiritual gifts that we didn't always understand, appreciate or respect in each other became the very characteristics we treasured.

The first time Julie saw a marked difference in the way she and Stan would react to situations, was when he stopped to give a man, laboring under the hood of a smoking engine, a helping hand; something she was never inclined to do. This scenario was played out again and again early in their marriage. And it was fine until kids entered their lives.

Julie wasn't too enthusiastic about Stan's kind-hearted *helps* gift with two helpless babies in the back seat. Her protective motherly instincts said, *"No, don't stop. You don't even know those guys!"* Two men were standing out by the road waving their arms for someone to rescue them, but Stan quickly stepped on the gas, reluctantly listening to Julie's panicked voice. It was the beginning of many misunderstandings until Julie and Stan saw each other's reactions as a blessing and gift from God.

Every believer in Jesus Christ has been given a spiritual gift (Ephesians 4:8). We're even told in I Corinthians 14:1 to earnestly desire spiritual gifts. When we learn about each other's gifts, not only can we understand why our spouse acts the way they do, but we can bring balance and wisdom to our own gifts. Our spouse's gifts can even rub off on us as we observe their strengths, making us even more effective for God's purposes.

Earlier, you heard about Barbi's lists. When we first got married, Barbi had pages of lists. She made lists in the form of outlines on the pages of her Bible; she had "To Do" lists for the next day; and she even wanted Terry to make lists with her every night before they went to bed. Well… this was just too much. The combination of her teaching and administrative gifts almost drove

Terry crazy. Understanding was needed, because some of these disagreeable traits were the very gifts God had given to her.

Now we both make lists, but not as rigidly as Barbi had done in the past. Over the years, as we've learned to listen to each other, we have more wisdom in the expression of our gifts. Every spiritual gift we have can get out of balance, and we need each other's input to use them effectively. There's no one better than our husband or wife to help us. As we are sensitive to understand each other's spiritual gifts, our love and commitment can grow.

If you are not sure what your spiritual gift is, a good Christian bookstore will have a number of materials that will assist you in finding out. So, the next time a missionary comes to your church and your spouse wants to write them a big support check, don't be too quick to stop them. *Giving* might be the very thing God has gifted them to do!

Look-up Scriptures:
Acts 1:4-8; 2:38-39   I Corinthians 12:27-31: 13:2
Acts 8:20-23; 10:44-48   I Tim. 4:14; II Tim. 1:6-7
Romans 12:4-8   James 1:17; I Peter 4:10-11

Questions to Ask Myself:
Do I know what my spiritual gift is? Am I willing to seek out a test that will let me know? Do I know what my mate's gift is? Am I giving them an opportunity to use this gift?

Questions to Ask Each Other:
Do you feel like we are giving each other an opportunity to use our spiritual gifts? How can we more effectively do this? 💣 Do you ever feel like I'm stifling the exercise of your spiritual gift?

Prayer: Lord, we thank you that it is YOU who gifts every believer with the gifts that will benefit the rest of the Body of Christ. Help us to be more understanding of our mate's gifting, and how to better allow them opportunity for expression of their gift. Thank you for the benefit that comes to our marriage through this gift you have given!

"We who are strong ought to bear with the failings of the weak and not to please ourselves." Romans 15:1

It has been said that "opposites attract." But some of us married a person whose background is so different from ours that it might take a lifetime to understand them. Occasionally, we may just have to agree to disagree until we see eye to eye. It takes time to resolve issues when we're coming from such different places.

Few couples have exactly the same background. Every marriage has potential differences in: religion, culture, parenting techniques, philosophies of life, socio-economic class, levels of education, etc. But regardless of our background, we <u>all</u> have something to offer that is of value to our mate.

Researchers studying *Autism* have found that those with the worst symptoms of this disorder can still display brilliance in an isolated area of their brain. Most of us are far from dealing with such challenges. But chances are, that even with a few quirks, YOU might display brilliance in some areas!

When we got married, we didn't realize how much our differences in background would affect us. One of us grew up in a conservative Christian home where parents were protective, and the other grew up with a good deal of freedom with very few rules and restrictions. Thankfully, we came to some agreement in our parenting styles (which were light years apart). We have learned to focus on the important things and love each other in spite of our differences. If we can't agree, it doesn't necessarily mean the other is wrong. We are just different.

Our upbringing makes an incredible impact on us, providing a template from which we frame our views on marriage, parenting, and overall worldview. Various traumas experienced in childhood make such an impact that we often subconsciously recreate them once we are married. Therapists who deal with victims of abuse know, that, despite the rejection and torment, an abused person will often gravitate toward another abuser – you'll often see a woman, having divorced an abusive man, get right back into an abusive relationship. Like a guided missile, they are attracted to this type of man again and again because of childhood experiences.

How do we break these awful cycles of destructive family patterns? Obviously, the most important place to start is to seek God and learn from the truths of His Word. But additionally, qualified, biblically sound Christian therapists and nurturing support groups can be of great help in ending dysfunctional behaviors. Many have found deep healing from their past through counseling, and some have even saved their marriages, by seeking competent people for help.

As we endeavor to understand our spouse and bridge the gaps created from our differences, God will empower us to remain faithfully committed. And, just remember, you might be brilliant!

Look-up Scriptures:
Romans 3:28-29   Romans 10:12-13   Galatians 2:6-16

Questions to Ask Myself:
What are the good things that I bring to marriage from my past? What are the things that are not so good? Am I willing to get biblically-based, professional counseling for things I can't change alone? Do I feel needlessly unworthy of God's grace because of my past, or do I know that God loves me and is not partial?

Questions to Ask Each Other:
♦※ Do you see some destructive patterns in my life that bear some resemblance to my past family background? Will you help me to change? Will you join with me in committing this area of need to daily prayer? If we are unable to change these cyclical family patterns, will you go with me to get professional help?

Prayer: Lord, we know that our family background has a great effect on us, even in our adult life. Help us to overcome the destructive patterns and habits that hurt our spouse and be willing to seek out help from those that specialize in these areas. May the cyclical family patterns we've inherited stop in our generation and not be passed on to our children, or any others in our family. We thank you for the blood of Jesus that was shed for all dysfunction, all destructive patterns, and the shame that often follows.

"… and a little child will lead them." Isaiah 11:6

Like Bill Murray in the movie, "Groundhog Day," we have had to learn the same lesson many times in different ways: Though God doesn't create junk, He can use anyone or anything to carry out His will. When He calls us to do something, we should never hesitate to obey. Occasionally we've thought, *"But she could do that much better than me!"* or *"Why me? I'm not so good at that."* or *"If I try it, I'll make a fool of myself."* While this may appear to be humility, underneath the religious veneer is a heart of pride.

In Matthew 28:19-20, Jesus said, *"Go and make disciples of all nations, baptizing them in the name of the Father and of the Son and of the Holy Spirit, and teaching them to obey everything I have commanded you."* At the end of this charge He doesn't add, *"…if you feel qualified."* Just the fact that He commands us to go qualifies us.

Then why are so many of us reluctant to do what Jesus said? Often, when we resist the Lord, it's because we fear people's rejection, or we think God is somehow dependent on our abilities. Of course, this is ludicrous. God even used a *donkey* to rebuke a prophet. Usually, at the very root of our hesitation is a lack of willingness to obey. When God commissions us to a task, we need to pray and find out how He wants us to fulfill the task, and then follow His direction.

You may already be doing something to obey God's commission to *"make disciples."* But we have a suggestion of how you can fulfill this mandate, while spending constructive and rewarding time with each other. If you don't have a plan, allow us to suggest one…

As we have researched ministries around the world and their effectiveness, we have found a common principle that works in discipleship more than any other: One on one, friendship evangelism and discipleship. This was how the early Church won the lost and discipled people. Few churches have ever grown as rapidly as the 1st century Church. There are many contemporary examples of one on one discipling that testify to the effectiveness of this approach. Some churches are seeing whole cities touched by married couples who are willing to reach out and coach other married couples.

As you have gone through this devotional study, we hope it has ministered to you and your marriage in some way. There are many useful materials you can add to your established reading and prayer habit now that you have completed this study. But may we suggest that you write down, in the back of this book, the names of couples (saved or unsaved) that you would like to see go through this devotional study, and coach them together? Now that you're off to a good start and are meeting together regularly, you could encourage some of your own friends to do the same. Perhaps their marriage could benefit from this devotional as well. More of these books are available either through your pastor, or our office.

Our hope is that we can bear much fruit around the world by multiplying the truths found in this book through YOU! You can share the Word of God with people we will never know!

Please take a moment right now to pause and ask the Lord how He would have you reach out to other couples that need encouragement. Pray for your friends and neighbors in the back of this book. Ask God to give you a heart for the world! If you have questions, please contact us at: www.heartfortheworld.com

Look-up Scriptures:

I Samuel 2:35

Mark 16:15-16

John 3:16

Romans 12:1-2

I Corinthians 1:18 - 2:8

II Corinthians 12:9-10; 13:4

Questions to Ask Myself:
Have I learned some new things about myself and my spouse in these last 40 days? Am I willing to continue meeting together?

Questions to Ask Each Other:
Do you feel like our communication has increased through this study? Can you think of other couples who might benefit from this study? (Take a moment to list them on the back page of this book.)

Prayer: Lord, Thank you for guiding us through these last 40 days. Help our love and romance to continue to grow! Reveal to us your plan as to how we can "make disciples" and help others.

❧ Recreational Survey ❧

Instructions: In the columns under *Husband* and *Wife* put a number between 1 (= least like), and 10 (= most like) next to each activity. When both of you are done, total your scores under the *Total* column at the right of the other two columns. Scores of 16 or more are your most mutually enjoyable activities. If you have never tried an activity, and you think you <u>might</u> like to try it, put a 6 or higher. If your spouse is interested in that recreation, you might find that you'd like it as well. If you don't like it, then try another activity that you both enjoy. You'll come up with your favorites… have fun!

Activity	Husband	Wife	TOTAL	Activity	Husband	Wife	TOTAL
Acting				Dancing			
Aerobics				Darts			
Amusement parks				Dining out			
Antique shopping				Dirt biking			
Archery				Fishing			
Astronomy				Flying			
Auto customizing				Football			
Auto racing				Four-wheeling			
Badminton				Gardening			
Ballet				Genealogy			
Baseball				Golfing			
Base jumping				Gymnastics			
Basketball				Ham radio			
Bible Study				Handball			
Bicycling				Hiking			
Board games				Hockey			
Boating				Home Remodeling			
Body building				Horseback riding			
Bowling				Horse shows			
Boxing				Horse racing			
Bridge				Horseshoe			
Bungee jumping				Hot air balloons			
Camping				Hunting			
Card games				Ice fishing			
Canoeing				Ice skating			
Checkers				Jogging			
Chess				Judo			
Church Ministry				Karate			
Coin collecting				Knitting			
Computer prog.				Metalwork			
Computer games				Model Building			
Concerts				Monopoly			
Cribbage				Motorcycling			
Croquet				Mountain climbing			

Movies	___	___	___	Skin diving	___	___	___
Museums	___	___	___	Skydiving	___	___	___
Musicals	___	___	___	Snorkeling	___	___	___
Opera	___	___	___	Snowboarding	___	___	___
Paint Ball	___	___	___	Snowmobiling	___	___	___
Painting	___	___	___	Softball	___	___	___
Parasailing	___	___	___	Spear fishing	___	___	___
Photography	___	___	___	Stamp collecting	___	___	___
Pistol shooting	___	___	___	Surfing	___	___	___
Plays	___	___	___	Swimming	___	___	___
Poetry	___	___	___	Table tennis	___	___	___
Polo	___	___	___	Taxidermy	___	___	___
Pool	___	___	___	Television	___	___	___
Pottery	___	___	___	Tennis	___	___	___
Quilting	___	___	___	Tobogganing	___	___	___
Racquetball	___	___	___	Trap shooting	___	___	___
Rock Collecting	___	___	___	Video games	___	___	___
Roller-skating	___	___	___	Video production	___	___	___
Rowing	___	___	___	Volleyball	___	___	___
Rummy	___	___	___	Wake boarding	___	___	___
Sailing	___	___	___	Weaving	___	___	___
Sculpting	___	___	___	Woodworking	___	___	___
Skeet shooting	___	___	___	Wrestling	___	___	___
Shopping	___	___	___	Yachting	___	___	___
Shuffleboard	___	___	___	_____	___	___	___
Sightseeing	___	___	___	_____	___	___	___
Singing	___	___	___	_____	___	___	___
Skiing (crss-cntry)	___	___	___	_____	___	___	___
Skiing (snow)	___	___	___	_____	___	___	___
Skiing (water)	___	___	___	_____	___	___	___

Below, list your mutually enjoyable recreational activities (with scores of 16 or higher), and put the TOTAL score in the column next to the activity below:

Mutually Enjoyable Activity	TOTAL	Mutually Enjoyable Activity	TOTAL
_____	___	_____	___
_____	___	_____	___
_____	___	_____	___
_____	___	_____	___
_____	___	_____	___
_____	___	_____	___
_____	___	_____	___

Now pick the activity you'd like to start with: **Activity:** _____

Write down the day that you want to do your first activity: **Day:** _____

Instructions: Each of you should choose your favorite chores and put your name beside them. Some of these items won't apply in your home, so you can adapt it to your circumstances and copy what works for you. As you start into another week, it's up to you if you want to switch your chores around. If there are things left over that no one wants... remember, pick something you believe will fill your husband's/ wife's love tank to increase romantic love and meet a need. Try to be encouraging to each other's hard work... we all want affirmation and appreciation for the work we do!

☺ *Indoor Work – weekly* ☺

NAME:

- ❑ **laundry:** (fold and distribute when done with each load please)
  - ❑ dark & bright colors - wash in cold water
  - ❑ medium colors & **faded** jeans only - wash in warm water
  - ❑ whites - wash in hot water (add a small amount of **bleach**)
  - ❑ pink towels - wash separately in **cold water**
  - ❑ green towels - wash separately in **cold water**
  - ❑ sheets - wash separately in cold water
- ❑ see grocery list & check
- ❑ clean bathroom sinks & vanity surfaces
- ❑ scrub toilets *with toilet bowl cleaner* (**including** base)
- ❑ scrub showers & tubs with a *soft abrasive cleaner*
- ❑ windows – use a *alcohol/water mix* or a window cleaner
- ❑ clean stainless trash can & refrigerator
- ❑ clean stove top with spray or soft abrasive cleaner
- ❑ scrub kitchen sink with abrasive cleaner
- ❑ wash all kitchen counter tops and table top
- ❑ spot clean carpets before vacuum
- ❑ vacuum all carpets (use *Upright*)
- ❑ vacuum all wood & tile floors & carpet edging
- ❑ vacuum stairway & throw rugs (use *hand held*)
- ❑ vacuum both return vents
- ❑ dust all horizontal wood surfaces (remove decorations)
- ❑ dust all other horizontal surfaces with dry cloth (picture frames too)
- ❑ dust all ceiling fans with fan duster
- ❑ mop all wood floors including front hall
- ❑ mop bathroom & sunroom tile floors

(Please feel free to copy these pages for your continual use.)

☺ *Outdoor Work – Weekly* ☺

NAME:

- ❑ Take trash cans to street (Wed PM)
- ❑ Take trash cans back to house (Thu PM)
- ❑ Mow lawn around house
- ❑ Mow field behind fence
- ❑ Weed whack – use string trimmer
- ❑ Blow off driveway
- ❑ Spray weeds – use "Round-up"
- ❑ Vacuum interior carpet of Mini-van (throw out trash)
- ❑ Replace all burned out flood lights
- ❑ Wash windows – inside and out
- ❑ Clip bushes
- ❑ Rake leaves
- ❑ Bring wood in for fireplace
- ❑ Wipe off and clean deck chairs & table
- ❑ Test pool water and add chemicals (do in early evening)

☺ *Daily Chores* ☺

Task:	NAME: Sun Mon Tue Wed Thu Fri Sat
unload dishes from dishwasher	
load dishes into dishwasher	
clean counters & table off	
empty trash into can outside	
clean rooms and put clothes away	
all personal items go to your room	
clean front hall and kitchen counter	
put away all food items use	
clean up after yourself after use	
cook dinner for family	
clean up dinner, food & dishes	

Tips for the Romantically Challenged Man

Some guys *want* to do something, but just don't know
where to start. Here are a few tips you can use as a guide:

Tip #1 – Make your wife feel special by doing something special.
   Idea: Find out what her schedule is and get a babysitter for an all night
stay at a nearby hotel. Don't pick the Motel 6. Pick a place you know is
reputable and is as nice as you can afford. Arrange and reserve a table for 2 in a
romantic restaurant near the hotel for a special intimate conversation and dinner.
On the way, you might even drop in at her favorite clothes or shoe store if you
know she loves shopping.

Tip #2 – Be secretive about your plans with her.
   Idea: Wives love to feel protected and cared for by their husbands.
Keeping things confidential and secret helps her feel freedom to express her love
for you. Give cell # for emergency calls only, but don't tell anyone where you'll
be. Sit close to her and whisper things into her ear during dinner. Listen to her
talk about whatever she wants to say. Ask her how she feels about those things.

Tip #3 – Show your admiration by watching her walk, talk, eat, etc.
   Idea: Wives still want to feel like they are attractive to you. If she
knows you're watching and enjoying her, it will light a spark inside. She'll be
even prettier from the inside out because she feels adored. You might even bring
a candle in her favorite scent (don't forget the matches) to light up the room a
little... just enough to see her when it's dark (in a hotel room or even in your
own bedroom).

Tip #4 – Spend time asking her what she thinks and then listen.
   Idea: Many times women feel inferior, depending on their life
experiences. Your wife will be thrilled that you care what SHE thinks about any
subject. She needs to feel like she is your partner and equal... that you are
genuinely interested in her perspective. You'll find out new things you enjoy
about her.

Tip #5 – Spare no expense on her.
   Idea: If you're a man that's always pinching pennies, this will be an
exciting detour for your wife. The Bible says that a righteous man is generous in
all his ways. What a great way to express your love... to bless her with the finest
things... a five course meal, real flowers, and delicious indulgences for this

special occasion. You could even prepare and present a specially wrapped single chocolate truffle right before the dessert and coffee is served to let her know you thought about her before the night began. (This will take planning ahead.)

Tip #6 – Appeal to all her senses.
   Idea: Arrange for a dozen red roses to be placed in your room before arrival... perhaps you can check in earlier in the day and arrange the room with fresh flowers. Touch her gently on the arm or cheek during dinner. Place your hand on the small of her back as you escort her. Have a CD and player ready for her favorite romantic music. Light some candles and set the music on low. Surprise her by trying to dance with her.

Tip #7 – Don't be in a hurry with her.
   Idea: Enjoy lingering and speaking softly to each other, sharing dreams, teasing, laughing about funny things you've experienced. Don't be forceful. Accept a single kiss or embrace as she warms up to you through the evening. Enjoy her. You may want to slip a love note in her purse the night before or call her at work to tell her you are looking forward to having dinner alone with her. When you see her, smile and take her hands. Look her in the eyes and gently kiss her lips.

Tip #8 – Be playful with her.
   Idea: Look for opportunities to be playful with your food and drink, or with clothes if you're shopping with her. Keep the evening lighthearted and fun. If you aren't normally playful, let her warm up to it, she'll start to get the idea and join in. If she's trying on shoes, kneel down and offer to put the shoe on for her... even rubbing her feet while you're doing it.

Tip #9 – Be accommodating but spontaneous with her.
   Idea: Lead your wife without being controlling or pushy. Seize the opportunities that come your way to be romantic. If things aren't going like you planned, you can abandon your plans for another time, but be confident and daring with her. Don't give up, she needs your affection!

Tip #10 – Surprise her with a gift.
   Idea: If all goes as planned, after dinner you may want to take her on a short walk across a lantern-lit plaza. Find a secluded spot and give her a small present (make it personal). You may even wait to surprise her till you walk into your room together. Make it thoughtful and creative. She'll **want** to open up and show her love and gratitude to you...

❧ *Resources for your Marriage* ❧

Protect your marriage and family from internet pornography with
our recommended filtering service found through www.afo.net

www.lifecoachinginternational.net specializes in
addictive/compulsive behaviors, including pornography addictions.

www.estherministries.org is a ministry that encourages wives
of those that struggle with addictive behaviors.

Dave Ramsey at www.financialpeace.com has many helpful tips, resource
materials, and a great plan to help you with financial management.

Crown Financial Ministries at www.crown.org specializes in equipping
people to learn, apply, and teach God's financial principles.

Resource and Counseling Options:

www.marriagebuilders.com   www.faithfamily.net

www.famtoday.com   www.steveandanniechapman.com

www.marriagesavers.org   www.turnbullministries.org

Resource Materials and Bibliography:
(Authors do not necessarily endorse all content of resources listed.)

What Husbands & Wives Aren't Telling Each Other, Steve & Annie Chapman,
Eugene, Oregon, Harvest House Publishers, 2003

Love Busters: Overcoming Habits that Destroy Romantic Love, Willard F.
Harley, Jr., Grand Rapids, Michigan, Revell (Baker Book House Co.), 1992

His Needs Her Needs: Building an Affair-Proof Marriage, Willard F. Harley,
Jr., Grand Rapids, Michigan, Revell (Baker Book House Co.), 1886

Hedges: Loving Your Marriage Enough to Protect It, Jerry B. Jenkins,
Brentwood, Tennessee, Wolgemuth & Hyatt, Publishers, Inc., 1989

Marriage On The Rock: God's Design for Your Dream Marriage, Jimmy
Evans, Amarillo, Texas, Majestic Media, 1994

Pure Desire, Ted Roberts, Ventura, California, Regal (a division of Gospel Light), 1999

The State of Affairs: Why The Happen, How Love Can Be Restored, Todd Mulliken, Mukilteo, Washington, WinePress Publishing, 1998

Lord, is it Warfare? Teach Me To Stand, Kay Arthur, Sisters, Oregon, Multnomah Books, 1991

Why Not Women? Loren Cunningham, and David J. Hamilton, Seattle, Washington, YWAM Publishing, 2000

The Subtle Power of Spiritual Abuse, David Johnson, and Jeff VanVonderen, Minneapolis, Minnesota, Bethany House Publishers, 1991

Reconcilable Differences, Healing for Troubled Marriages, Jim Talley, Nashville, Tennessee, Thomas Nelson Publishers, 1991

De Recte Fide ad Arcadiam et Marinam, Cyril of Alexandria, Cyrilli Opera 1.1.5 5(2).63 (ed. Pusey), vol. 7, pt. 1, 182

Teaching Science in a Climate of Controversy, David Price, John L. Wiester, and Walter R. Hearn, Ipswich, Mass., American Scientific Affiliation, 1993

The Basic Works of Aristotle, Aristotle, Trans. Richard McKeon "Politics 1.12.1259, a-b." New York, Random House, 1941

Subordination in the Godhead: A Re-emerging Heresy, Dr. Gilbert Bilezikian, Wheaton, Illinois, transcript of lecture, 1993

The New Brown-Driver-Briggs-Gesenius Hebrew-English Lexicon, Francis Brown, Peabody: Hendrickson, N.d., 1979 by J. P. Green, Sr.

Clergy Couples in Crisis, The Impact of Stress on Pastoral Marriages, Dean Merrill, Waco, Texas, Word Books Publisher, 1985

Nicene and Post-Nicene Fathers of the Christian Church, Philip Schaff, and Henry Wace, Eds., 1st & 2nd Series, Grand Rapids, Mich, Eerdmans, 1978.

The Handbook for Spiritual Warfare, Dr. Ed Murphy, Ed., Revised and Updated Edition, Nashville, Tennessee, Thomas Nelson Publishers, Inc., 1992, 1996

A Greek-English Lexicon of the New Testament, John Henry Thayer, 4th ed., Milford: Mott Media, 1982, 225

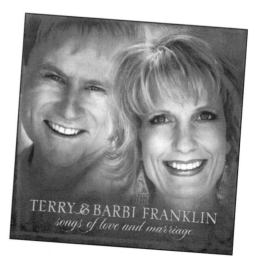

Terry & Barbi Franklin have been in Marriage & Family Concert and Seminar ministry since 1985. They have ministered in over 34 countries around the world with the outreach ministry they founded, "Heart For The World." Having a passion to see marriages strengthened and families united by the power of God's Word and the work of the Holy Spirit, Terry & Barbi believe that the world can be changed... by changed families. Their theme since 1990 has been, "Inspiring Love in the Home & Revival in the Church."

In 20 years of traveling, they have ministered to congregations of every major denomination in over 6000 churches around the globe. Terry & Barbi have personally seen the truths of God's Word bring countless marriages and families closer together. This compilation of devotional writings (with audio listening CDs) was inspired by conversations with thousands of ministers and their wives, counselors, marriage therapists, and couples the Franklins have counseled, as well as personal stories from their own lives. This study guide is packed with powerful truths and interactive questions that will fill and change your heart... and quite possibly, change your marriage forever.

If you have never received God's free gift of salvation, we encourage you to take a moment right now to ask Him to be your Savior and Lord. Romans 10:9-10 says, "That if you confess with your mouth, 'Jesus is Lord,' and believe in your heart that God raised him from the dead, you will be saved. For it is with your heart that you believe and are justified, and it is with your mouth that you confess and are saved." Pray the prayer below, from your heart, to commit your life to Jesus. You will not be disappointed!

PRAYER OF SALVATION:
Dear Jesus,

I confess that I am a sinner and have broken Your law. I choose, this day, to place all my trust in the payment that You, the sinless, perfect One, made for me on the Cross when You died and rose again. I give You my heart and my life. Please liveYour life through me. Amen.

Please list the couples that you want to pray for and encourage:

_____   _____

_____   _____

_____   _____